Imagining a Sermon

IMAGINING A SERMON

THOMAS H. TROEGER

Abingdon Press

Nashville

Imagining a Sermon

Copyright © 1990 by Thomas H. Troeger

This book is printed on acid-free paper.

Library of Congress Cataloging-in-Publication Data

Troeger, Thomas H., 1945–
  Imagining a sermon / Thomas H. Troeger.
    p. cm. — (Abingdon preacher's library)
  Includes bibliographical references.
  ISBN 0-687-18694-3 (alk. paper)
  1. Preaching. 2. Imagination—Religious aspects—Christianity.
I. Title. II. Series.
BV4211.2.T764   1990
251'.01-dc20

                       89-28379
                         CIP

Figure 1, p. 54, and Figure 2, p. 56, are from *Sacred Texts of the World* by
Othmar Keel. Copyright © 1978 by The Crossroad Publishing Company.
Reprinted by permission.

"The Leper's Soul Was No Less Scarred," pp. 58-59, and "These Things Did
Thomas Count as Real," page 97, reprinted from *New Hymns for the Lectionary*
by Carol Doran and Thomas H. Troeger. Copyright © 1986 by Oxford
University Press. Reprinted by permission.

"The Negro Speaks of Rivers," pp. 132-33, copyright 1926 by Alfred A.
Knopf, Inc. and renewed 1954 by Langston Hughes. Reprinted from *Selected
Poems of Langston Hughes*, by permission of Alfred A. Knopf, Inc.

Scripture quotations are from the Revised Standard Version of the Bible,
copyright 1946, 1952, 1971 by the Division of Christian Education of the
National Council of Churches of Christ in the USA. Used by permission.

MANUFACTURED IN THE UNITED STATES OF AMERICA

For
Susan
Reaves
Stephen
Victor
Sally
Brenda
Darryl

ACKNOWLEDGMENTS

This book was originally delivered as the Schaff Lectures at Pittsburgh Theological Seminary in April, 1988. I give special thanks to my excellent hosts, Professor Richard Oman and his wife, Mary Ellen. I also thank Jeanette Rapp, Director of Continuing Education, who gracefully handled administrative details. I also want to remember Mary Alice Schaff and the Reverend David Kaminsky, who welcomed me to the First Presbyterian Church in Youngstown, Ohio, to repeat part of these lectures for the congregation.

CONTENTS

IMAGINING A SERMON

CHAPTER 1

*H*ow Preachers Can Become More Imaginative

An idea for a sermon flashes across your mind. You jot it down and start writing. For a moment the sermon flows. Then unforeseen difficulties become apparent, your creative energies fade, and you wonder whether the original idea was worthwhile in the first place.

The pattern is familiar to most preachers. Imagination can be as capricious as the wind, whirling ideas and images about the mind, then falling as still as the air on a breathless day. After the initial gusts of inspiration blow themselves out, we face the hard labor of discovering the meaning of that revelation, which promised so much when it first seized our thoughts.

Perhaps that is part of the attraction of many traditional homiletical systems; they provide a plan for digging a sermon out of our minds when we do not feel inspired. There is something reassuring about having a logical, step-by-step method. I consider, for example, Cicero (106–43 B.C.), whose classic work *De Inventione* has had a continuing impact on Western Christian homiletics. The process is so clear that it seems that a preacher could construct something to say no matter how cold and dry the wells of inspiration are.

> Invention is the reasoning out of truth, or that which
> is like the truth, to make a case probable. Arrangement
> is the orderly distribution of what has been found. Style
> is the fitting of suitable words to what has been found.
> Memory is a firm grasp in the mind of subjects and
> words. Delivery, or pronuntiatio, is the control of voice
> and body suitable to the subject and the words.[1]

Is it possible to make the elements of using a
preacher's imagination as lucid as the components of
classical rhetoric? To put the matter the way most of
my students do: Can I learn to be more imaginative? I
face this question again and again, not only with the
seminarians I teach, but also with pastors who come
to workshops and tell me that they are tired of their
own preaching, that they want to be more creative
but are uncertain of how to accomplish their goal.
They are eager to learn because week after week they
see the importance of the imagination in preaching
effectively to an age whose consciousness is shaped
by the mass media.

Yes, we can learn to be more imaginative.

The imagination is not purely capricious. If we
analyze those moments of inspiration when our
hearts and minds take fire, we discover that there are
patterns of experience and reflection that encourage
the imagination. Its activity is not random and
chaotic. The imagination has principles of its own.
Imagination is what Paul Ricoeur calls "a *rule-go-
verned* form of invention (alternatively, is norm-go-
verned productivity.) This disallows any purely
Romantic understanding."[2]

The imaginative process can be compared to the art
of sailing a boat: We cannot make the wind blow, but
we can trim the sails and tend the helm. We cannot
compel the Spirit to fill our imaginations with wind

and fire, but we can practice those disciplines of prayer and thought that will open us to God's revelations.

A Surprising Principle

What, then, are the principles for using our imaginations so that we can receive the *ruach*, the Spirit of the living God to whom our preaching is a witness? The primary principle from which all the others are derived is that we are attentive to what is.

That principle may surprise us. Common understanding has it that imagination is fickle and fanciful, dealing more with dreams and visions than with actuality. But if we examine the imaginative work of artists and poets, we discover that they have drawn the raw materials of their creativity from close observation. They have been attentive to how the dawn light suffuses the air, how the snow balances on a bough, how a bird rides on the wind, how everyday speech has a music all its own.

When we are attentive to what is, we do not gum up our consciousness with preconceptions that remove us from the truth of our experience. We trust, as did the biblical writers, that common things may be the source of revelation.

And the Lord said to me, "Amos, what do you see?"
And I said, "A plumb line." Then the Lord said,
   "Behold, I am setting a plumb line
      in the midst of my people Israel.
      I will never again pass by them. . . .
"Amos, what do you see?" And I said, "A basket of summer fruit." Then the Lord said to me,

> "The end has come upon my
>   people Israel;
>   I will never again pass by them."
> (Amos 7:8, 8:2)

Preacher, what do you see? Not just as you read this book but as you live day by day. If it is not plumb lines and baskets of fruit and the images of an ancient, agrarian world, what do you see? What world emerges from your daily routines and the mass media that shape the public understanding of culture and politics? What images and events could you draw upon to vitalize your imagination? *Preacher, what do you see?*

Theological Reflection on Remote Control

I roll over in bed and press the power button on my television remote control. I see people on the screen who are making disgusted faces as they look at the dishwasher powder that has caked on their glasses and plates. They toss the crystal and dishes over their shoulders out the windows to shatter on the ground. Then they form a circle and dance to celebrate the liquid detergent that leaves everything sparkling.

Next a scruffy looking western outlaw, ready to draw his gun, meets a smiling Scandinavian who presents him with a "pick-me-up bouquet." The gunslinger decides to forego the shoot-out and smiles a toothy grin.

The local station flashes its call letters, and then I see the first video news shot: several bodies lying in blood on a street, with a voice-over telling where it happened this time, followed by an end zone shot of the last big play at the Superbowl. The news anchor announces, "These are our top stories this morning. . . . " As the reporter speaks, I notice a poster in the crowd that can be seen through the goalposts: **John 3:16.**

. I wonder how many viewers catch sight of the sign. Of those who do, how many know that it refers to a verse in the Bible? I would not be surprised to learn that there are people who think John 3:16 is the code for a play that some fan wants the quarterback to call.

My hunch is that the people who are most apt to see the sign are those who already know the verse: "For God so loved the world that he gave his only Son, that whoever believes in him should not perish but have eternal life."

Preacher, what do you see?

I see the world God loves: the people who are upset about the dishwasher powder caked on their glassware; the tough outlaw smiling to receive a bouquet; the six who lie dead in puddles of their own blood from a terrorist ambush; the tight end who manages to come down with the ball and the two defenders who scissor him in leaping tackles from opposite sides; all the fans who cheer and boo; and those tenacious believers who gathered magic markers and poster board to make a religious poster to hold up in a stadium before millions of television viewers, who are also included in the world that God loves.

Paul the apostle wrote: "But how are [people] to call upon him in whom they have not believed? And how are they to believe in him of whom they have never heard? And how are they to hear without a preacher?" (Rom. 10:14). Now I would add: "And how is the preacher to be heard by people who begin their day pressing the power button on their remote controls?'' The answer begins with paying attention to the mass media images that are shaping people's imaginative worlds. The question—*Preacher, what do you see?*—is an invitation to observe that world with critical eyes.

While the television anchor reads in an upbeat tone this morning's quotient of terror, tragedy, and leading market indicators, I am remembering that I have several extra sermons to preach in the coming weeks. Lent is approaching, and I have committed myself to holding a service with a sermon every Wednesday evening. I have a wedding next weekend, and the couple have requested that I preach on the meaning of covenant. I have gotten as far as looking up the Ash Wednesday lection from Joel 2. I do not remember the exact words, but their images have left a shadow on my consciousness. They go something like:

> Blow a trumpet in Zion.
> Sound an alarm.
> A day of blackness and gloom is coming.
> "Rend your hearts and not your garments."
> Gather together everyone from nursing children to grooms and brides.

I have thought hard about what to preach, but nothing has come yet. I keep hoping for the Spirit to stir my imagination with a strong wind, but all is quiet and still. I want what I preach to matter, but my words seem too meager for the task. I fear that God's word will be as lost in my people's lives as that poster, John 3:16, was in the midst of the cheering stadium crowd during the Superbowl.

My eyes travel back to the tube, where a news story

on starvation is followed by a commercial for a luxury car, which drives off toward a beautiful mountain, which gives way to a woman in a sweat suit telling a middle aged man why he needs a high fiber cereal before we hear the weather report. A blast of cold arctic air is shown on the national map as a cartoon cloud with billowing cheeks. The cheerful advice of the meteorologist to ''bundle up when you go out'' gives no indication that many people are already out there on the sidewalks and in cardboard cartons in the back alleys, where they have been all night.

Blow a trumpet in Zion, sound an alarm, do something to dispel this cheery glibness that denies what we need to face. Thinking of Joel's command to sound the trumpet and call a solemn assembly brings to mind a statue of two angels that I once saw in a church in Europe.

Preacher, what do you see? Notice how the question and my attentiveness to the visual world awaken scenes from my memory. This commonly happens when we take time to look carefully at what is. For many preachers, it can be the first step in activating their imaginations.

Preacher, what do you see? I see those angels in the church. One angel with puffed out cheeks is blowing a great long trumpet, and the other stands waiting to read a long, uncurled scroll as soon as the trumpet player has finished sounding the alarm. The remembrance of the angels gives my heart a lift, and from the beat of my pulse arise a few simple rhythmic lines:

Sound the trumpet,
Sound the trumpet,
Sound the trumpet yet again.

Sound the trumpet,
Sound the trumpet,
Let the solemn fast begin.

But no trumpet sounds on the television screen. Instead, someone is sprinting through the halls of an executive office building and down the street, energized by the paroxysms of a Big Mac attack.

Preacher, what do you see? The question has now touched off various levels of consciousness so that televised, scriptural, and remembered images are linked in associative patterns. These patterns are what charge us with visionary energy when the imagination strikes with power. Only, in this case, I am not waiting for it to strike; I am nurturing its energies by attending to the images I see and remember without prematurely trying to come up with a sermon outline.

One of my favorite commercials comes on the screen while I am dressing. I stop tying my tie to watch. I will not tell you exactly which commercial it is because it would be more productive for you to imagine the one you most enjoy. The commercial that catches my heart every time I see it is a little human drama, thirty seconds in duration, that suggests with brief dialogue and telling glances the lifetime relationship of the two characters. Through them I recall a similar scene from my own life. I already own the product that the commercial is selling, a different brand that I have no intention of changing. Nevertheless, I keep watching. When the commercial ends, I hit the power button on the remote control and go down to breakfast while my head swims with memories that were awakened by a commercial for a product I do not need.

Video Replay in the Preacher's Head

A little later in my attic study, that favorite commercial is on video replay in my head while I try to think of a way of understanding homiletics that would be as effective for our age as classical rhetoric was for the early church. I look at the large table in the center of my study where I have piled dozens of books that I have read during the last few years, as well as those I have recently taken out of the seminary library to prepare sermons and classes. The stacks of books look like a model city of skyscrapers, a metropolis of homiletical wisdom built by biblical scholars, theologians, poets, literary critics, media analysts, novelists, and visual artists, some of them going back centuries and some of them very new inhabitants.

While the images of morning television continue to flicker in my consciousness, I reach into the city and pull out Peter G. Horsfield's *Religious Television: The American Experience* and reread a quotation that has haunted me since I first read it a few years ago:

> Far from being merely a neutral communication medium, television in America has become an integrated symbolic world filling the socially functional role demanded of it both by its viewers and its advertisers. . . . William Fore, the Assistant Secretary for Communication in the National Council of Churches of Christ, suggests that there are several other dominant myths in television programming that are of direct relevance for religious broadcasters. These myths are:
>
> —The fittest survive
> —Happiness consists of limitless material acquisition
> —Consumption is inherently good

—Property, wealth, and power are more important
  than people
—Progress is an inherent good.

> Fore asserts that "the whole weight of Christian
> history, thought and teaching stands diametrically
> opposed to the media world and its values."[3]

Preacher, what do you see? Horsfield and Fore
identify why that question is essential for the pulpit
today. We need to proclaim the gospel with a
vividness that will challenge the world of the media
and its values. Such a perspective would also affirm
those times when the media promote community,
justice, health, and peace.

I have never forgotten an observation that Alistair
Cooke made in introducing a dramatic episode about
World War I. He said that if the war had received the
same televised front line coverage that Vietnam later
would, then the horror in the trenches might have
destroyed the romanticized imagery that surrounded
and sustained the conflict, and the parties might
have come to the negotiating table. In a similar way, I
know people who have been stirred to action by vivid
television reports of starvation, the plight of AIDS
victims, the problems of the homeless, and the
devastations of family violence.

But even as I consider these positive uses of the
media, the morning television images rebroadcast
themselves in my head:

> the dance for liquid dishwasher detergent;
> the western outlaw receiving a bouquet;
> the ambush victims in their blood;
> the winning touchdown;
> John 3:16;

the story on starvation, giving way to the luxury car;
followed by the high fiber diet;
and then my favorite commercial.

I turn again to the city of books and pick up a volume that earlier in this century was a standard item in many homiletics courses: P. T. Forsyth's *Positive Preaching and Modern Mind.* Published in 1907, when there was no broadcasting industry, the book reveals a far different understanding of the relative strengths of the pulpit and the press.

> The pulpit has a Word, the press has none. The pulpit has a common message and, on the strength of it, a claim, while the press has no claim to anything but external freedom of opinion and expression. The one has a Gospel which is the source of its liberty, the other has no Gospel but liberty, which in itself is no Gospel at all. . . . The press is there for information, or for suggestion at most, it is not there for authority; but the pulpit is there with authority; and the news it brings is brought for the sake of the authority.[4]

Even if Forsyth's claim for the neutrality of the press is overstated, what he describes is radically different from the mass media of our age and what Fore describes as its "integrated symbolic world." Television, the movies, home videos, and the slick photo magazines that report on the stars of the media world *do* have a gospel and *do* represent authority—strong authority.

Finding Help in the City of Homiletical Wisdom

While the video replays continue in my head, I take out my Bible to read the Ash Wednesday passage from Joel:

Blow the trumpet in Zion;
  sound the alarm on my holy
    mountain!
Let all the inhabitants of the land
    tremble,
  for the day of the Lord is coming,
    it is near,
a day of darkness and gloom,
  a day of clouds and thick
    darkness!
Like blackness there is spread upon
    the mountains
  a great and powerful people;
their like has never been from of old,
  nor will be again after them
  through the years of all
    generations. . . .

Blow the trumpet in Zion;
  sanctify a fast;
call a solemn assembly;
  gather the people.
Sanctify the congregation;
  assemble the elders;
gather the children,
  even nursing infants.
Let the bridegroom leave his room
  and the bride her chamber.

Between the vestibule and the altar
  let the priests, the ministers of
    the Lord, weep
and say, "Spare thy people, O Lord,
  and make not thy heritage a
    reproach,
  a byword among the nations.

Why should they say among the
    peoples,
  'Where is their God?' "
(Joel 2:1-2, 15-17)

I turn to the city of homiletical wisdom spread out
on my table and find a lectionary study aid by Pheme
Perkins. I read: "Since Joel is not speaking in a time of
national political emergency, we are to see this
national repentance as an acknowledgment of
fundamental truths about God embodied in the
covenant traditions and the prophetic heritage."[5] I
gaze out a window of my study to the city streets and
the skyscrapers; cars go by, and there is no sense of
emergency.

I allow myself to daydream, to juxtapose the
images of my environment with what I am learning
from scholars. I do not wait to collect all my data and
then engage my imagination. Instead, I weave back
and forth between reading and daydreaming, sometimes seriously, sometimes playfully considering the
links between scholarship and our task as preachers.

I turn back to my commentary on Joel: "This
passage also reminds us that repentance is not
response to an obvious evil or time of national crisis,
but is grounded in a knowledge of the nature of God
and of God's fruitful love for a people who can never
claim to have deserved such mercy."[6] I put the book
down and think of what such repentance would
mean for mass media culture. I keep switching
channels in my head between the televised images of
the morning and the prophet's cry: *Sound a trumpet in
Zion.* Joel does not give us an easy score to play. We
preachers better begin trumpet practice for Lent. We
have a difficult part to master, a theme that will

sound dissonant and harsh compared to the dance for the dishwasher detergent and the music for the luxury car that zooms toward the beautiful mountain.

Imaginative Theology

I replay the entire morning in my mind. I begin to see that my flow of consciousness in dialogue with the Scripture and the city of homiletical wisdom is revealing the shape and substance of my Ash Wednesday sermon. I have been allowing the images of Joel to disturb the assumed world of the media and the city outside my dormer window. That is how I have heard the prophet's trumpet, and that is how the congregation can hear the trumpet when I preach.

I have been practicing "imaginative theology." Imaginative theology employs the visionary and integrative capacities of the mind to create theological understanding. It uses the powers of observation to become receptive to the Holy Spirit, who works upon our consciousness through patterns of association and juxtaposition.

Imaginative theology in the pulpit utilizes those patterns to evoke similar reflections in the listeners. That is what I have done with you, the reader, sharing the creative process in order to awaken your own. Although I need to refine and clarify my sermon on Joel, the message and outline are manifest in the process itself. I will not cheat the congregation by handing them a souvenir from my trip on the river when I can take them along on the voyage and let them feel the current and the water for themselves.

Too many sermons hide the preacher's imaginative work so that listeners receive the impression that when God's word comes it arrives in a hermetically sealed tube. This has the effect of discouraging listeners from their own theological reflection. Imaginative theology is a way of helping them to use their processes of consciousness to interpret what faith in God means for them day by day.

Facing Reality

I turn from Joel to consider each of the subsequent texts for the season. Usually, I would not cram so much into my head at once because I like to let my mind play with one passage at a time. But I promised a theme for Lent, some fresh way of approaching the season.

Those listeners who prefer a more logical approach to understanding their religion will appreciate a clear statement of principle. Congregations, like seminary faculties, have their own systematic theologians, listeners who, though they do not call themselves by that title, are eager for a rational account of the faith. Although that is not my dominant way of approaching reality, I know that if I think through the implications of my intuitions and visions, a reasonable principle may emerge because, as Wordsworth observed, imagination is not the opposite of reason. Quite to the contrary; imagination is

clearest insight, amplitude of mind,
And Reason in her most exalted mood.
(William Wordsworth, from *The Prelude*)

As I continue in the exalted mood of letting the images of the Lenten lectionary flow through me, I try to feel the direction of the current of theological thought. This is what strikes me as I read the lections: In every case the biblical writer is helping us to face something our culture tends to deny. On Ash Wednesday, Joel's trumpet disrupts our self-satisfaction and demands that we acknowledge our utter dependence on God. Every Sunday after that, the readings confront us with more and more of reality—our need to repent, to deal with suffering and death, to realize how facilely we accept and then reject Jesus, and to see how in the name of religion itself we may hide from God.

We preachers have to practice playing Joel's trumpet because our culture conspires to suppress the truth we are called to announce. A name for the Lenten series comes to me: "Sounding Joel's Trumpet: Facing What Our Culture Denies." The first half of the title will appeal to the poets and the second half to the philosophers.

I repeat the Lenten title to myself and reflect on how we commonly associate the imagination with illusion and deception. "It is all in your imagination," we say. But imagination is leading us to an acknowledgment of reality, not an escape from it. Of course, it is not imagination on its own, but imagination encouraged by the Spirit, disciplined by Scripture, informed by the wisdom of the homiletical city, and energized by the need of the world.

Shifting Models for Preaching

Before the domination of the mass media, when oratory and later print were the sovereign forms of communication, it was natural that homiletics should draw its rules and norms from classical rhetoric. The city of homiletical wisdom is filled with instruction about

the clarity of the argument;
the logic of the outline;
the tightness of the transitions;
the development of the main point;
the persuasiveness of the reasoning;
how well the illustrations fit the principles;
and the theological defensibility of the message.

Although these principles remain helpful for preachers, the model of homiletics is changing. Just as systematic theology reveals "the shift from the speculative reason of classical patristic, medieval and later idealist theologies to the more troubled, more modest reflections of the post-Kantian critical reason of modern theologies,"[7] so, too, does homiletics give evidence of transforming its models and hence its rules and norms for creativity.

What lies before us in the city of homiletical wisdom is the witness of centuries of struggle to interpret God's word to particular people living in particular times and places. Now we must be equally bold to name the principles that can guide us in creating sermons for our time and place.

From the experience of listening to hundreds of preachers, I have formulated seven principles for the practice of imaginative theology:

1. Alert the eye to keener sight.
2. Feel the bodily weight of truth.
3. Listen to the music of speech.
4. Draw parables from life.
5. Understand the church's resistance to imagination.

6. Dream of new worlds.
7. Return to the Source.

Each of these expands the implications of our first principle—be attentive to what is—and each of these is the central topic of a subsequent chapter.

Some students have suggested that the rules and norms for imaginative theology reflect various theories of the brain and psyche, such as the balance of left and right hemispheric thinking or neurolinguistic programming, which claims that we all have a dominant language system for processing reality—aural, visual, or bodily. Such theories may or may not be sustained by future research. I believe that a more lasting basis for these rules and norms lies in the character of our being—namely, that we have been created to know, love, and serve God with all that we are, with heart and soul and mind and strength. That belief is the source of my conviction about imaginative theology and my inspiration for praying:

God, give me the confidence to trust
in the way you have created me,
so that I may use all that I am
to be attentive to what is
and may thereby learn
how to awaken in my listeners
the same compassion and justice
which was in Christ Jesus, Amen.

Notes

1. This concise summary of Cicero's process is from George A. Kennedy, *Classical Rhetoric and Its Christian and Secular Tradition from Ancient to Modern Times* (Chapel Hill: The University of North Carolina Press, 1980), p. 92.

2. David Tracy, *The Analogical Imagination: Christian Theology and the Culture of Pluralism* (New York: Crossroad Publishing Company, 1981), p. 149. Tracy is summarizing in his own words an unpublished lecture of Ricoeur's. Emphasis is Tracy's.

3. Peter G. Horsfield, *Religious Television: The American Experience* (New York: Longman Inc., 1984), pp. 47-48. The quotation that is cited is from William F. Fore, "Mass Media's Mythic World: At Odds with Christian Values," *Christian Century* (January 19, 1977): 34-35.

4. P. T. Forsyth, *Positive Preaching and Modern Mind*, p. 43.

5. Pheme Perkins, *Proclamation 3: Aids for Interpreting the Lessons of the Church Year, Lent* (Philadelphia: Fortress Press, 1985), p. 9.

6. Ibid., pp. 10-11.

7. Tracy, *The Analogical Imagination*, p. 411.

CHAPTER 2

*A*lert the Eye
to Keener Sight

The untrained eye is not adept at seeing things accurately. How easy it is to look without observing, to let verbal preconceptions obscure our vision so that we fail to feed our hearts with images that can vitalize our preaching.

Over the years I have assigned theological students the task of finding a piece of art for a Good Friday bulletin cover. They were to bring the picture to class along with a brief meditation on the artist's work that would be appropriate for typing on the back of the bulletin cover.

One student wrote a meditation on the peace and courage we could see in the face of the Savior as he bore the cross to Calvary. But when we looked closely at the face of Christ in the picture, we noticed that the eyes were dilated, like those of a trapped animal, and the fine muscles at the corners of the mouth and eyes were drawn tense by pain so that the face looked about to crack under the strain. The student's preconceived verbal ideas distorted his ability to see what the artist had actually drawn. The result was a subjective projection that blocked the accurate use of the imagination.

Refining Our Visionary Powers

The first task for this student as a preacher was to learn to see the world more accurately until he was able, as Rudolph Arnheim has said, "to understand through the eyes."[1]

Margaret Miles describes a three-step discipline by which we may begin to train our eyes:

1. Become aware of the messages we receive from the images with which we live.
2. Assess how those images are shaping our political and social perspective.
3. Develop a repertoire of images that help us to envision the transformation of life.[2]

From the moment I hit the power button on my television remote control, I have been attempting to embody these principles in the practice of my homiletic. If what I have done seems overwhelming to you, then break the process down into more accessible units. Look at a still picture and study a single character in it.

What is the play of light and shadow on the face?
Where do the eyes focus?
Are the lips tight or relaxed?
How is the head held? Resting on a hand? Tilted sideways? Chin up or down?
What is the posture of the shoulders?
What details of the picture are in the character's range of sight?
What details are beyond the character's perspective?

Ask more questions. Answer them with graphic descriptions, so exact that persons who see the picture after reading your words will immediately identify what you have observed.

Parallel your repertoire of still graphic images with a selection of television commercials. If you own a VCR, collect a series of advertisements from prime-time viewing, replay them and analyze the gospel or the anti-gospel that is present in them.

How would you broadcast the gospel to your people in a thirty-second spot? If you can write out such a commercial, you will have the beginnings of a highly effective sermon. If you are not working with a picture but a passage of Scripture that involves a scene, organize the sermon so that it describes the spatial relationships of the setting and the characters.

Where is the road?
Where is the mountain?
Where is the light?
Where is the crowd?
How will your gestures and glances suggest the location of these things to the congregation?

Use visual details not only to create your sermons but also to critique them. Can the listener see your sermon? In asking such a question, you are doing more than exploring a homiletical technique to make your sermons engaging. You are asking a question about dimensions of reality that are significant for our understanding and expression of the whole truth of God. The opening chapter of the Bible reminds us again and again that God delights in *seeing* creation: "And God saw that it was good." To help people see in a sermon is not only a way of engaging them as listeners, but it is also a way of affirming the biblical affirmation of the goodness of creation.

Generations of Print and the World of Images

I am a member of the last generation in this country to be introduced to books before television, so words and print had a primary place in my life prior to the broadcast image. I recall the first television in our neighborhood, owned by our friends next door. I was in second grade. The set featured a six-by-six-inch tube in a big cabinet. Its images were nearly overpowered by the well waxed wood that framed its fuzzy gray and white images of Howdy Doody. It seemed a dull edition of the much brighter picture books that were read to me as a child, and had it not been for the novelty of the thing, I am not sure that I would have watched as much as I did.

The fact that my primary language as a child was verbal and not visual continues to influence me several years later as a preacher. For example, when I sit down to write a wedding homily on covenant for a couple who met with me last night, the first thing that occurs to me is not some highly imaginative sermon, but a classic rhetorical statement.

It will be the groom's second marriage and the bride's first. He has a sense of failure over his divorce. Both of them are eager to make this new marriage a lifelong commitment. I am touched by them, by their earnest desire to keep the vow they will make: "I promise and covenant to be your loving and faithful [wife/husband] for richer for poorer, for better for worse, in sickness and in health as long as we both shall live."

I awakened before dawn this morning to write the sermon while last night's conversation is still fresh and stirring my creative energies. I find that my remembrance of the couple intermingles with scenes from the television show that my wife and I watched before we went off to sleep. The plot for each major scene was the same: people either shoot each other or go to bed with each other.

I gaze upon the books that rise from my study table, and I think of the infinite distance between what I watched on the screen as I went to sleep and the hopes of the homiletical city and the best yearnings of that couple with whom I spoke last night. Their young friends will be at that wedding, many of whom, they told me, are only in church on special occasions. They do not belong to the generation of print, but to the new world of sight—the mass media age. Theologies of covenant and faithfulness are at best faint echoes in their minds, compared to their vivid acquaintance with "Dallas," "Dynasty," "L.A. Law" and the offerings of HBO and videotapes.

The jagged beat of the music that accompanied the most violent scenes on last night's show echoes in my head, its rhythms reminding me what stiff competition the word of God will face at that wedding. The shows, if you count the reruns, are on all year. My sermon will be brief: a homily of about five to seven minutes.

The Best Desires of the Human Heart

But there are resources in the situation that I must not forget. There is the power of ritual and symbolic action to touch people at the deepest point in their being. All humans need to pray just as they need to breathe and eat. No matter how bruising life has been, most of them, including the couple's young friends, hold on to the hope that people can live up to a promise of fidelity and love. God has made us for such a life. Therefore, even if the culture denies that sacred possibility through its daily images of sex and violence, the best desires of the human heart can be awakened by a word of truth.

Because I believe this, I am a preacher.

Because I believe this, I am sitting here in my study, praying and reflecting in the early morning. I look out the skylight and see that the moon is still in the crown of the great silver maple tree. Its slivered shape looks like the curve of some partially illuminated heart that is pumping light down through the vein-like branches of the tree to the roots, which extend beneath the foundation of my house from where they send up emanations to my attic study. I feel part of a great capillary system that circulates truth from heaven to the earth through the city about me and the city of books on my desk and the couple I will marry and the congregation who, if they are moved to pray, will complete the cycle of spiritual energy through their act of praise.

I turn to the homiletical city, looking for a resource to structure the flow of feeling that is animating my imagination so that I can shape my insights into a sermon for the wedding. I consider some of the marriage texts that have been used again and again at weddings: the opening chapters of Genesis, the wedding at Cana, Paul's hymn to love. I am eager to settle down and get the thing done.

A Sample Rhetorical Sermon for the Print Generation

I turn on my word processor and decide that since I have only a few minutes for the homily, I will step directly into the theme in the first sentence.

In a few moments, Catherine and Jonathan will repeat their vows: "I promise and covenant before God and these witnesses to be your faithful and loving wife/husband for better for worse, for richer for poorer, in sickness and in health as long as we both shall live."
Promise and covenant—*what antique words these are to our ears. They sound like something we might find carved in Romanesque letters on a stone monument or written with indelible ink on vellum, bearing an official seal.*
Promise and covenant—*they are not the words of everyday speech. They are not the words we use during coffee break or on the street or talking across the fence with our neighbor.*
Promise and covenant—*these are sacred words. When a couple speaks them in a wedding service they set loose once again the voices of*

Abraham and Sarah;
Moses and the prophets;
the apostles and the martyrs.

They remind us that God has made a promise to us: to guide us, to support us, to love us, to hold us to account for how we live. And we have made a promise to God: to be faithful, to do justice, to show compassion, to witness to our faith in Jesus Christ.

Promise *and* covenant—*these are words that are deeper than feeling. That idea is hard for us to grasp. In our society, there is a tendency to reduce everything to what an individual feels. But feelings alone are an inadequate foundation for a marriage. If I feel I love you today, I may feel different tomorrow.*

Promise *and* covenant *do not change with our moods. When we promise and covenant, we make a commitment, a pledge, to be faithful partners to each other no matter what happens—for better for worse, for richer for poorer, in sickness and in health.*

Promise *and* covenant—*for the rest of your lives remember these sacred words, these words rooted in the promises of God, these words that go deeper than feeling.*

Remember them in the night when a child cries.

Remember them when bitter speech has passed between you.

Remember them when your bodies fail from illness or age.

Remember that you spoke these words to each other.

In the remembering, hear again the voice of One who loves you with an everlasting love and who will supply the grace and strength to keep the promise and covenant that you are making this day.

I stop and read the sermon off the screen of my word processor. I am not pleased with it. It sounds too talky for the generation of television viewers who will be present. The sermon depends on old rhetorical devices: the repetition of a phrase, allusions to the Bible, and an exhortation at the end. It is not that all of this is bad or wrong, but it lacks what television has conditioned the congregation to expect: immediacy, vividness, and a fast-paced plot.

For a minute I console myself that those qualities are antithetical to the message I am preaching, and what I have on the screen is perfectly all right. I scan the homiletical city, thinking about where I might find justification for such a sermon. I turn to George A. Kennedy's work on classical rhetoric and read his summation of the six parts of a public speech from Cicero's *De Inventione*:

—the exordium: prepares the audience, makes them attentive and receptive
—the narration: sets out the basic case to be made
—the partition: a statement of agreements and disagreements with opponents
—the confirmation: we make our case
—the refutation: the falseness of opposing positions is shown
—the conclusion or peroration: a summary, inciting indignation against the opponents and winning sympathy for the speaker.[3]

I turn back to my sermon and note that almost all of Cicero's elements are present in my brief homily. I prepare the audience and set out the basic case in the opening paragraph. I make a case for promise and covenant, contrast it with opposing views from popular culture, and conclude with a peroration on the importance of remembering the vow. Perhaps I should tell the congregation that what they are about to hear is Ciceronian.

The Stress of Biblical Illiteracy

But then I realize that they do not know who Cicero is. I will be happy if they catch my reference to "Abraham and Sarah, Moses and the prophets, the apostles and the martyrs." I can no longer assume that biblical names are common knowledge among young people.

Last spring I was preaching to eight hundred Boy Scouts at a camp jamboree. I was drawing on stories from my own mountain climbing experience and from journey passages in the Bible. The Scouts were following me attentively (I could see it in their faces) until I happened to mention in passing "David and Goliath." It was simply a phrase to clarify some other part of my sermon. But I saw many faces go blank, saying to me: "Who are David and Goliath? You did not mention them before." So I had to make an instant detour in that sermon, working in the story of David and Goliath and then picking up where I had left off.

Now I worry that the same thing will happen at the wedding. I will speak the names "Abraham and Sarah" and look out at blank faces that are asking, "Who are they, relatives of the groom or the bride?"

Peter S. Hawkins, a relatively new inhabitant in my homiletical city, is right when he observes that "the whole theological frame of reference, concretely expressed in Scripture, that once provided the coherence for Western culture and imagination . . . does so no longer."[4] The rich use of biblical allusions, which earlier generations of preachers employed to give their sermons a holy resonance, is no longer available to me. There is a burden now on the preacher to carry the weight of the scriptural witness without help from the culture. I am feeling that burden right now in my study. And for a moment I grow resentful of mass culture and its loss of contact with what was good and true in the past.

Many articles have been written about burnout among the clergy. They usually address things like time management and the stress on ministers' families. Not for a moment would I deny these realities. But I sometimes think the greater cause is the spiritual exhaustion that develops as ministers realize the enormous gap between the gospel and the culture, the incessant tide of images, fads, and fashions that threatens to wash away the church's witness.

Creating Sermons with Electronic Alphabet Noodles

I sense that tide now as I read through my wedding homily. The message seems as insubstantial as the print on the screen of my word processor. Those phosphorescent words appear as nothing more than electronic alphabet noodles that I have flicked up from the darkness with the touch of a finger. How different from ancient days, when things were impressed in clay tablets or carved in stone. When Jeremiah proclaimed that the law would be cut on the heart (Jer. 31:31-34), his words must have branded the mind of the listeners. But now what are words? We do not cut, carve, or even write them. We process them. Words have become blips on the screen that vanish to blankness when the power is shut off. Words are the jingle that accompanies the commercial. Words are the fifteen-second sound byte that is all we hear from the candidate on the evening news.

Yet here I sit early in the morning, searching for words. The moon has moved out of the crown of the silver maple tree and is fading away. My eyes stare at the brightening blue of heaven, and the outward mysteries of dawn suffuse my imagination with a deeper light that leads me to ask: What images complement the ideas I have presented in my rhetorical sermon?

If I were a television producer who wanted to show the principle of covenant in action, I would not be able to stand on the screen and repeat my sermon as it is. The young people would switch channels, and they will do the same inside themselves if all I do is gab about covenant at the wedding.

I reread my initial homily, this time asking myself every few sentences: How can I telecast what I have said rhetorically? A sermon begins to broadcast itself in my head, and my fingers strike the keyboard, casting electronic alphabet noodles onto the screen of my word processor.

A Sample Visual Sermon for the Mass Media Generation

I once met a couple who told me that every anniversary they donned their wedding clothes and had their picture taken in the living room of their house. They planned to do this throughout their life together and to collect the photographs in a single album.

As you, Catherine and Jonathan, stand before this congregation in your wedding clothes, I am remembering that other couple. I imagine them on their fifth anniversary, coming down to the living room for their annual picture. She is in her white gown, and he is wearing his three-piece suit and formal tie. They are waiting for their next door neighbor who has gone to get some extra flashcubes.

The first four years, they hired a professional photographer, but this has not been a good year for them financially. The husband lost his job. The wife is only able to get part-time employment, and their second child is having medical problems.

Finally, their neighbor arrives. He positions them in front of the fireplace and suggests they hold hands, the way they did when they said their vows, the way you, Catherine and Jonathan, will do in a few minutes when you say yours.

While their friend fidgets with the focus, the wife notices the stuffing that is coming out of the sofa and wishes they had money to redo it. The husband sees their daughter's broken doll and thinks of one he saw in a shop window but could not afford.

Flash! "That's picture number one," says their friend.

While he steps back for another angle, the wife says to the husband, "Do you remember our vows? We memorized them."

They think a minute, then slowly repeat together: "I promise and covenant before God and these witnesses to be your faithful and loving wife/husband [the two words sound at once] for better for worse, for richer for poorer. . . ."

Poorer. The word bursts like the flashcube on their friend's camera and highlights the stack of bills on the table beneath the phone and the calendar marked with doctor's appointments they cannot afford. A look leaps between them.

"We promised."

The camera flashes again.

"That will be a good one," exclaims their friend.

Next I picture the couple ten years later. Things are much better for them financially. The husband has a good job. The wife went back to school and has just taken an excellent position. The colonial love seats by the fireplace have been recovered in a quilted chintz. Each of the children has a ten-speed bicycle in the garage.

But the husband and wife have thrown acid words at each

other. The second child, after all those trips to the doctor, is in trouble. Each partner has said to the other: "If you were not so preoccupied with your job and could give some time to the family, then things would be different."

On their fifteenth anniversary they come home and say they are too tired to get into the old wedding clothes. Then they remember that the photographer is coming in twenty minutes and has probably already left her studio and will charge them for the visit no matter what. So they trek up to the attic and throw themselves into the musty clothes, discovering that they have to suck in to get the zippers shut.

The doorbell rings.

The photographer comes in and takes control. "Come on now. Hold hands. A smile for the camera."

While the photographer clicks away, they get lost in the moment and begin to repeat the vow: "I do promise and covenant before God and these witnesses to be your loving and faithful wife/husband for better for worse. . . . "

Worse *flashes as brightly as* **poorer** *did ten years before, and again the look leaps between them:* "We promised."

Finally I picture their forty-seventh anniversary. They do not know whether they will make it to their fiftieth. He has had two heart attacks, and her hands are crooked with arthritis. Their granddaughter, herself engaged, is upstairs bringing down the old clothes. The dress has yellowed, and when the wife puts it on she tears a seam. The husband cannot get the trousers zippered, but if the picture is from the waist up and he buttons the coat, it will be all right.

He takes his wife's hands, her knuckles swollen and knobby, and out of their faltering bodies arises in a whisper the sacred pledge: "I do covenant before God and these witnesses to be your faithful and loving wife/husband for better for worse, for richer for poorer, in sickness and in health until death do us part."

In sickness . . . until death. . . . *Words that had slipped easily out of their mouths on their wedding day are now heavy with meaning.*

"I've got to go upstairs for more film," says the granddaughter.

But they are not listening. In looking into each other's eyes, they see something more beautiful than the prize pictures in their anniversary album: the grace and the glory of a promise kept.

That is our prayer for you, Catherine and Jonathan, that for better for worse, for richer for poorer, in sickness and in health, until death do you part, you may know the grace and the glory of a promise kept. May God, who has made an everlasting covenant with us, grant you the strength to keep your covenant for a lifetime.

Comparing the Two Sermons

I read the second sermon through from beginning to end, and begin nodding yes to what I have written. Behind my back is the city of homiletical wisdom that rises up on the table in the middle of my study. As I read, I have a strange feeling that the inhabitants of the homiletical city are looking out of their buildings, gazing over my shoulder at the print on my screen. Some are pleased with what I have written, and some wonder if it really is a sermon. I can almost hear them urging me to preach the first one instead.

I think I need to preach the second sermon, but the traditionalists in the homiletical city sound loudly in my heart. So I run both sermons off my printer, then place them side-by-side on the counter to compare their methods.

The second version of the sermon uses the flash of

a camera to make the transition from scene to scene. It is a cinemographic technique, which includes leaping through spans of time without the sustained development of a logical argument. The cumulative development of the sermon depends on tracing the life cycle and the evocations of feeling and insight awakened by observing the couple as they age.

The first version of the sermon keeps expanding the definition of the phrase "promise and covenant." The higher reliance on conceptualization leads to a more didactic and argumentative style: I build a case for the traditional marriage vow as opposed to simply feeling in love.

Yet, each sermon draws on the methods of the other. The second sermon relies on the rhetorical technique of repetition. The constant restatement of the wedding vow is the backbone of the sermon. And the conclusion even provides a small peroration of sorts: "May God, who has made an everlasting covenant with us, grant you the strength to keep your covenant for a lifetime."

In a similar fashion, the more rhetorical sermon uses many of the methods of imaginative theology. It employs images and scenes: words "carved in Romanesque letters on a stone monument," the child crying in the night, the bitter words, and the frailties of old age. In the rhetorical sermon, however, the images illustrate a principle that has already been announced. They are examples of the generalized truth in practice. But in the second sermon the images bear the meaning of the sermon rather than illustrate it. The result is a qualitative difference in the effect and tone of the two sermons.

When I finish comparing them, I still have not made up my mind about which to preach. I am drawn to the second sermon, but I keep remembering my childhood experience of preaching, which continues to influence my ideas of how a sermon ought to sound. I grew up listening to sermons—excellent sermons—that followed in spirit, if not detail, Cicero's tight structure. I am not alone in this. A congregation member once told me that, as a child in confirmation class, he had to be prepared every Sunday afternoon to repeat to the pastor the three points of the morning sermon. The assignment never varied because the sermon structure never varied. We may laugh, but there was value in such a homiletic. It taught the people who listened week after week that it was possible, and indeed necessary, to think in an orderly way about the Christian faith.

There is still need for sharply reasoned preaching in the pulpit! In the light of that need, perhaps I should deliver the first sermon. The clear thought of its logical outline would counter our society's propensity to reduce everything to feeling. Choosing a classical style could be part of a strategy to present the gospel as an alternative to the dominant psychological consciousness of our culture.

A Deeper Purpose for Imaginative Preaching

By the time I sit down to write the rest of this chapter, the wedding has come and gone. I preached the sermon that followed the principle of imaginative theology rather than Ciceronian rhetoric. While I was preaching, the mother of the bride turned pale.

Before the service, I had been certain of my choice. The story of the couple repeating their vows had illuminated my own marriage, and I have discovered from listening to hundreds of preachers that the best sermons are often those they preach *to* themselves. Note how I put that: not sermons *about* themselves, but sermons *to* themselves, sermons that address the fundamental realities of their humanity and that, therefore, speak to other human beings.

Although the mother of the bride appeared to be upset, other members of the congregation, including the youthful wedding party, were unusually attentive. People did not fidget as they often do, indicating their impatience to get through the sermon and on to the vows and the reception that would follow. Instead, I looked out at a sea of faces that were following every word.

Later, at the reception, when the formality began to fade and people moved around to different tables, the mother of the bride sought me out for a personal conversation. She explained that when I started the sermon, she remembered that her daughter had told her several weeks earlier that I would preach on covenant. This news had alarmed the mother because two members of her own family, a sister and a cousin, were just coming out of divorces. Knowing they would be present, she feared that the sermon might hurt them. She had intended to call me and discuss the possibility of my toning things down a bit so as not to hurt their feelings. But she never got around to the phone call. As the scenario of the sermon became clear, she had nearly fainted for fear of its impact on these relatives for whom she cared very much.

As the mother spoke, my first internal reaction was to think that I had not been sensitive enough to those in the congregation who were divorced. Maybe if I had gone with the rhetorical sermon, the ideas would have seemed more distant and less threatening. I had thought at one point of introducing something about divorce, but then I considered the couple's great desire to affirm their central hope for an enduring marriage. They had been clear about the need for a sermon on covenant.

I also recalled a minister who had recently tried to take into account the feelings of divorced members of the congregation during a wedding homily. Divorced, married, and single listeners later expressed their disappointment because no matter what their personal circumstance, they were looking to the church to hold up the vision of what marriage is intended to be.

All these thoughts flashed through my mind as the mother of the bride and I continued to talk. She went on to say that during the reception the cousin and sister had each spoken to her individually, explaining how moved they were by the sermon. It had made plain what their hopes were if they were ever to remarry. They were even more grateful because their teenaged children, who had been in the pews with them, initiated conversation about the sermon during the car ride from the church to the reception. Cousin and sister both explained that their children's positive responses to the sermon had made it possible to talk about things they had always wanted to say, but had never been able to.

I stood there dazed, trying to figure out how to preach God's word to a visually responsive generation and at the same time be sensitive to the various needs in a congregation. Then it struck me that maybe sensitivity and the imaginative proclamation of the gospel are not one and the same thing. Sensitivity is a social grace, highly favored in our society, which means to respect other people's feelings. Reasonably sensitive person that I am, if the mother had called me, her words would have affected me. But then I might have failed to touch the need in the heart to hear once more the promise of what marriage is intended to be. Sensitivity to feelings might have made me insensitive to the hope that was alive not only in the couple who were being married, but also in their relatives who were divorcing.

Somewhere near the end of the conversation with the bride's mother, she poured us both a dribble of champagne that was left in a bottle on the table. Raising her glass, she said, "Thank you." I returned the toast, giving thanks for what had happened and for the mother's graciousness in telling me the story. When I sipped the bubbly beverage, it tasted to me like wine from the wedding feast at Cana, and I saw with great clarity that the purpose of alerting the eyes to keener sight and using imagination in the pulpit is not simply to identify the listeners' feelings, but to envision the hope and faith in their hearts, which they may reclaim for their lives if the preacher declares them boldly.

Notes

1. Quoted by Margaret Miles, *Image as Insight* (Boston: Beacon Press, 1985), p. 152.

2. Ibid., pp. 147ff.

3. George A. Kennedy, *Classical Rhetoric and Its Christian and Secular Tradition from Ancient to Modern Times* (Chapel Hill: The University of North Carolina Press, 1980), pp. 92-94; provides a full description of these.

4. Peter S. Hawkins, *The Language of Grace* (Cambridge, Mass.: Cowley Publications, 1983), p. 1.

CHAPTER 3

*F*eel the Bodily Weight of Truth

Truth that matters to us has a physical impact on our bodies. When, for example, grandparents take up grandchildren in their arms, they forget their recent grumblings that it is getting harder to pick up a bag of potatoes in the grocery store. The truth of love pours strength into joints that are stiff and muscles that have lost their tone. The truth of joy awakens energy that they thought they no longer possessed.

Sometimes, depending on the nature of the truth, we experience the opposite effect: our stomachs knot, our fists clinch, our shoulders bend under the burden. But whether joyful or saddening, truth that matters has a bodily weight, a physical force on our animal frames. This should come as no surprise to Christians, who believe that "the Word became flesh," not a cloud or a thought but flesh, a human being.

How can our preaching communicate the bodily weight of truth? How can our words stir the tangible energy of belief that filled the shepherds who ran to see the Word made flesh, the child born in the middle of the night?

The Material Experience of What We See

Before we preach convincingly of the incarnation, we must be aware of the physicality of our life as creatures. Having alerted the eye to keener sight, we need to feel the bodily weight of the truth we would declare. One way to learn to do this is to enter the material experience of what we see.

Take, for example, figure 1, an Egyptian sketch on limestone, New Kingdom (1570–1085 B.C.). The image comes from Othmar Keel's *Sacred Texts of the World.* The author observes how the bowed figure keeps one knee drawn up because the position of complete abasement is "not a sustained posture, especially not in daily practice." Before God we know we are dust; yet, by grace we need not remain in that state.[1]

The visual simultaneity of the various postures in the picture suggests their interrelationship: we can stand tall because we have bowed low. In depending totally on God bowing, we receive strength to act responsibly in our lives standing. The picture expresses the tension that lies at the center of our lives as religious beings— namely, "How does one lean on God and give over everything to Him and still stand on his [or her] own feet as a passionate human being?"[2]

I enter the material experience of the picture by bowing

and standing myself and allowing the bodily weight of the truth to set loose the words of a prayer.

> This day O Lord, I bow low to you,
>   I bow to your wonder and your glory,
>   to your everlasting love.
> And by your power I stand tall,
>   tall for the truth,
>   tall for the gospel,
>   for justice and compassion.
> I bow low and stand tall.
> And in my bowing and my standing,
>   I know your grace. Amen.

The prayer is stirring me to thought, and the thought will eventually lead to a sermon. If I am a wise preacher, I will not simply report the final essence of my thought. I will employ language that helps the listeners to feel the bodily weight of the truth, to experience bowing and standing, leaning on God and being the self-responsible people they are called to be.

Logosomatic Language

Keel relates the Egyptian figures to the following verses from the Bible:

> O come, let us worship and bow
>   down,
>   let us kneel before the Lord, our
>   Maker!
> (Ps. 95:6)

And to Psalm 29:2b: "Bow down to Yahweh when the Holy One appears." Notice how many words involving bodily action are used in the text: *come, worship* (meaning "prostrate oneself" in Hebrew), *bow,* and *kneel.* The language is nearly as vivid as the drawing! I call this form of speaking "logosomatic" language, because it proceeds from the creative ordering power of reality, the *logos,* as it works in and through our bodily (*somatic*) existence.

The iconographic environment of the ancient Near East reveals the logosomatic quality of much biblical language. Because such language is close to the nerve and bone of being human, it helps us to experience the bodily weight of truth.

We are aware of the need to make this weight tangible when we search for a prop for a children's sermon. Children will grasp through an object what they cannot reach through a concept. One of the many reasons adults often prefer children's sermons

is that these sermons make manifest the bodily weight of the truth, so that the gospel does not seem abstract and distant.

Consider figure 2, an image from Mesopotamia, Ur III Period (2050–1950) in which an intercessory figure leads a worshiper by the hand before an enthroned God.[3] Think of the need small children have for someone to lead them into a dark or strange place. You could use this picture on a bulletin cover and speak to both children and adults at various levels of meaning.

The Mesopotamian image portrays the human fear of what is unknown and mysterious, a fear that the writer of Hebrews addresses by transforming the intercessory imagery into vivid logosomatic language:

> Since then we have a great high priest who has passed through the heavens, Jesus, the Son of God, let us hold fast our confession. For we have not a high priest who is unable to sympathize with our weaknesses, but one who in every respect has been tempted as we are, yet without sin. Let us then with confidence draw near to the throne of grace, that we may receive mercy and find grace to help in time of need. (Heb. 4:14-16)

The contemplation of the Mesopotamian image and the behavior of children empower me to see the logosomatic dimensions of the biblical passage. The presence of Christ becomes less heady and more immediate. I sense that Christ, like the intercessory figure in the icon, takes me by the hand and goes before me.

To heighten the logosomatic character of your own speech, adopt the posture and expression of the biblical figure you are describing. If you are blind, shut your eyes. If you are deaf, plug your ears, or at least turn off all appliances and sit in the quietest room you can find. If you are paralyzed, sit or lie down without moving. Do not worry about getting the right words too quickly. Hold the posture for a while. Let your body tell you the words of need. Then if there is a healing in the passage, and you finally begin to see or hear or move, let the words arise from the materiality of the experience.

Primary Reality

In reading a text, we do not automatically arrive at a level of primary reality. Our reflective consciousness tends to supply premature interpretations that protect us from the experience that has been condensed into the text and that awaits release through the church's proclamation.

I recall, for example, what happened when I first tried to write a hymn on Christ's healing the leper in Mark 1:40-45. My initial efforts were too abstract. I used Latinate words like *alienation, rejection* and *estrangement,* words that distance us from the bodily weight of the leper's experience and Christ's physical touch. Only when I began to see myself as the leper, listening to the words of those who rejected me and finally rubbing my face with my hands and thinking of them as Christ's hands, only then did the logosomatic language begin to stir in my brain. Here are the opening stanzas:

> The leper's soul was no less scarred
> Than were his face and skin.
> The curse, "Unclean, unclean!" had marred
> God's image deep within.

No hands had grasped his hands for years,
  No lips had kissed his own,
No greeting came his way but jeers
  And looks of ice and stone.

Then Jesus stroked the leper's cheek
  And swept the sores away
But charged the man he should not speak
  Of what took place that day.[4]

If I were to develop the poem into a sermon, I might at some later point employ the abstract words with which I started—*alienation, rejection, estrangement*. But now these terms would have behind them primary reality, the flesh and blood, the heft of logosomatic language: "No hands had grasped his hands for years/ No lips had kissed his own."

Incarnate Truth

The bodily weight of truth is what we celebrate in Christ's birth: "The word became flesh." Our goal as preachers is greater than offering people interesting ideas about life and death. We want them to know God, who identifies not only with our thoughts but also with our breath and our pulse beat, our muscle and our bone. This is why we are training our imaginations to feel the bodily weight of truth.

I felt the tangible force of the incarnation with renewed power when a human rights group asked me to preach during the season of Christmas. They requested a sermon about the congregation's need to act on behalf of the victims of political persecution.

I was initially tempted to use the sermon to report statistics and information that I knew about the topic.

But through conversations with the group and my own personal reflection, I decided that the more important goal of the sermon was to work on the theological and motivational level of the congregation. A display of literature and an education period would be the means of information.

No other Christian celebration blends the truth and the distortion of the gospel more thoroughly than Christmas. All the warm and sentimental images that surround the season were an inescapable factor in anticipating how listeners would receive a sermon on violations of human rights. Certain images and feelings are so precious to most people that it would be a self-defeating strategy to attack them. In violating what is honored in their souls, I would lose my authority to speak against other human violations.

I began to consider how the warmth and the childlike wonder of the Christmas season arise from the profoundest need in the human heart: to know that we are cared for, to trust that God is with us in facing the pain and ambiguity of being human. This deep spiritual need springs from the same place in the heart as our ability to identify with those who suffer. Therefore, the warm human associations of the season, which preachers too often devalue, might help the congregation to identify with the victims of human rights violations, who need to know that they are not abandoned and are not without hope. The sermon, I decided, would honor the listeners' seasonal expectations while expanding their perception from the warm personal meanings of Christ's birth to its larger political dimensions.

Although my definition of the task drew heavily on rational analysis, I realized that a discursive sermon would be lost amid the carols, the candles, and the scent of the wreaths. I thought of how people picture Christmas in their hearts. Manger scenes started to fill my head. I turned to my books of Rembrandt paintings and etchings, knowing that his art often combines the warmth that believers prize with an unsentimental realism about the world and the gospel. When I looked at his painting of Joseph's dream in Bethlehem, I knew I had found the image I needed.

I now began to study the picture, examining its detail as closely as I had read Matthew 2:13-15. I stepped into the picture by adopting the poses of the various characters. I held those poses and felt the weight of what they were facing in my body, always having in the back of my mind the bruised and broken bodies of those who are being tortured around the world. A holy terror descended upon my heart and a sermon began to form within me.

A Sample Sermon

Mary is a round-faced peasant woman
　　leaning up against the manger
　　　　her eyelids
　　　　　　closed.
The shadow on her face suggests
　　a new mother whose energy
　　　　is sapped
　　　　　　by immediate demands
　　　　　　and future fears.
Her left arm
　　is slouched around the child on the hay.

Joseph sits a few feet to the side.
  A walking stick props up his right knee
  which props up his right forearm
  which props up his drooping head.
If a wind blows through the stable and topples him over,
  he will go on sleeping in the same posture on his side.
Emerging from the center of the picture
  with graceful, arching wings
    is an angel.
The angel has one hand on Joseph's shoulder
  and is leaning over to whisper a message.

I say to the angel:
  "Shhh,
    let them sleep.
      Can't you see they need their rest?"
But the angel does not listen to me.
  Heaven is too realistic about earth's brutality
    to keep quiet:
"Rise, Joseph!
  Take the child and his mother,
    and flee to Egypt,
      and remain there till I tell you;
      for Herod is about to search for the child,
      to destroy him."

The human rights policy of Herod's administration is clear:
  Herod claims all the rights
  to do with human beings
  whatever will keep him in power.
A voice shall be heard in Ramah,
  "wailing and loud lamentation,
    Rachel weeping for her children."
A voice shall be heard in
  Poland,

South Africa,
  Central America,
    Northern Ireland—
"wailing and loud lamentation,
  Rachel weeping for her children."

I look again into the sleepy stable.
  God's own child
won't live long enough to cut his baby teeth
  if Joseph and Mary don't wake up and act.

I call out:
  "Mary,
Joseph,
wake up!
Didn't you hear the angel?
  I know you are tired.
  You have every reason to be.
But the salvation of the world
  is depending on you.
    If you don't act,
      God's newborn love won't have a chance.
Rise.
Take the child.
Now."

Then I become still,
  shocked by my own words,
    "the salvation of the world is depending on you."
    Our salvation depends on this sleepy couple?
Would God be foolish enough
  to let heaven's purpose hang
    on such a fragile human link—
as fragile as Mary slouched around the manger,

as fragile as Joseph with his head propped in his hand,
  as fragile as you and me,
with bags beneath our eyes from too much partying
  and our bodies thick and slow
    from too much rich food?

        Yes.
        God is that foolish.
Wherever God's truth,
  wherever God's justice,
    wherever God's love
      wherever God's children
        are being born,
only a fragile human link preserves them from destruction.

I look once more into the sleepy stable.
  I hear a sound on the streets outside,
    several blocks away.
      The rumble of wagons
        and the beat of soldiers' boots,
          in step and implacable.
I call to the sleeping carpenter:
  "Wake up.
    Now."
He does not stir.
  The boots stop.
    Silence.
      A baby cries down the street.
        Again silence.
          Then I hear a woman
            wailing
            wailing
            wailing.
The boots begin again
  to mark their measured step.

"Wake up, Joseph!
  Wake up, Mary!
    For the love of God,
      wake up!
        Now."[5]

The Weight of Truth in the Preacher's Own Life

As I reread the sermon in my study, I hear God speaking to me in a way I did not realize when I first wrote it some time ago. Listening again to earlier sermons is an important part of tending to the work of the Spirit upon the preacher's imagination. It is not enough simply to analyze last week's sermon. Preachers need to keep going back over larger spans of time to see what their dominant patterns are, to know what is strong and what needs correcting, to see whether they have gotten hooked on one way of imaging God or humanity, to listen for promptings from the Spirit that they may have missed in the weekly rush of preparation, and to feel the bodily weight of truth in their own lives.

I feel that weight when I review the Rembrandt sermon and find myself stopping cold at the lines:

Would God be foolish enough
  to let heaven's purpose hang
    on such a fragile human link—

Through my own words, I hear God saying to me and to every preacher receptive to hearing: *You are a fragile human link. But I am depending on you not to cover up the terrors of this world. When you are tempted to lighten the bodily weight of the truth, remember Mary and Joseph. What if they had told the angel: "We are too tired to pick up* the child and get moving." *I have the same promise for you that I had for them and for everyone else I have called: I will be with you. My name is Emmanuel, not God-over-you or God-against-you, but God-with-you and I will help you bear the bodily weight of the truth in your own life and in your preaching.*

Notes

1. Othmar Keel, *Sacred Texts of the World* (New York: Crossroad, 1978), fig. 412. The work is a gold mine of beautifully done line drawings from wall reliefs and the like. Because of their boldness, they reproduce beautifully for bulletin covers. You will, of course, need to write for permission to do this. But it would be wonderful if the publishers of the book would give permission for some company to bring out a series of bulletins based on these images. This would be utilizing the church's scholarship in the most helpful way to preachers and liturgists.

2. Ernest Becker, *The Denial of Death* (New York: The Free Press, 1973), p. 259.

3. Keel, *Sacred Texts of the World*, fig. 412.

4. Carol Doran and Thomas H. Troeger, "The Leper's Soul Was no Less Scarred." In *New Hymns for the Lectionary: To Glorify the Maker's Name* (New York: Oxford University Press, 1986), p. 54.

5. I delivered this sermon to an Academy of Homiletics meeting at Princeton Theological Seminary. Although I was not able to reproduce the painting as I would have liked for the bulletin cover, a student of mine made a simple wordless banner with the bold symbols of manger and star, which reinforced the vivid quality of the sermon. It is not necessary in such preaching to have elaborate props. In fact, simplicity is often more effective since it leaves more to the listener's imagination.

CHAPTER 4

*L*isten to the Music of Speech

Our first step in training the imagination has involved becoming attentive to what is. Each subsequent principle is an expansion of that first one. So far we have been attentive with our eyes and our bodies. Now we want to listen to the music of speech with our ears.

I have saved this principle until now because we too often think only in terms of language when we want to revitalize our religious imagination for the pulpit. This strategy often fails because without fresh sources of experience, we fall back into our old ways of thinking and expressing ourselves.

Alerting the eyes to keener sight and feeling the bodily weight of truth can draw new language out of us, language that has the sparkle and energy of conversational speech. Listen to the contrast between the analytical sections of this book and those portions that capture the flow of consciousness and that are shaped into sermons and poems.

The physical properties of speech—its rhythm, pitch, volume, and inflection—are a kind of music that makes the imagination dance. Ancient peoples were aware of the special powers of speech, and they became anxious that the invention of writing would lead to the atrophy of memory and a reduction of wisdom because people would externalize their knowledge on the page instead of imparting it to their minds and hearts. In Plato's dialogue *Phaedrus*, Teuth brings his invention of print before Thamus, the king of Egypt, who warns:

> this invention will produce forgetfulness in the minds of those who learn to use it, because they will not practice their memory. Their trust in writing, produced by external characters which are not part of themselves, will discourage the use of their own memories within them. You have invented an elixir not of memory, but of reminding; and you offer your pupils the appearance of wisdom, not true wisdom, for they will read many things without instruction and will therefore seem to know many things, when they are for the most part ignorant and hard to get along with since they are not wise, but only appear wise.[1]

The truth of Thamus' judgment has become apparent to me in working with many preachers. I ask them to tell me what they want to preach, and they immediately cast their eyes to a sheet of paper. Their vocal quality and gestures become constricted, and the music of their speech flattens to a drone. They act out unintentionally what happened when print became a major medium of communication: "With the triumph of the alphabet, the melody of words necessarily became a less central aspect of some kinds of literature."[2]

The Melody of Words as a Witness to God

Yet, it is the "melody of words" that engages us in spoken speech. The lift, the lilt, the beat, the intensities, and the softenings of speech convey the truth that is forever greater than our words. We value speech because its aural properties suggest the ineffable character of personhood and the source of being from whom that personhood springs. Preaching will never die because a witness to the precise personal center of reality—God—is most effective when we receive it through a medium that expresses the fullness and wonder of what personality is, and that is accomplished more completely by speech than by the written word.

This does not mean that all preachers must preach without a manuscript. I have heard preachers who use a manuscript in such a fashion that the written sermon does not flatten their voices into prosaic reading tones, and I have heard those who speak without notes of any kind fall into a lifeless intonation that conveys no sense of the Spirit. Whether to use a manuscript or not must be settled on the basis of individual talents and predilections.

The more profound theological issue is that the voice of the preacher gives witness to the wonder and ineffability of God by being alive with the wonder and ineffability of human personality as expressed by the best physical qualities of spoken language. This requires training more than the eye and the body. We need to discipline the ear as well so that we may become aware of the aural effect of speech. A preacher whose ear is alert to the sound of spoken language may produce a manuscript that "preaches well," that breathes and pulses with the rhythms of the best conversational speech.

Training the Ear

The training of the ear concerned Robert Frost when he taught people how to read and to write:

The ear is the only true writer and the only true reader. I
have known people who could read without hearing the
sentence sounds and they were the fastest readers. Eye
readers we call them. They can get the meaning by glances.
But they are bad readers because they miss the best part of
what a good writer puts into his work.[3]

A preacher who reads the Bible only for meaning
will likewise miss the power of the cadences and the
imagery, which are as important as the exposition to
many listeners. This is borne out by the attachment
that many church members have to the King James
Version of the Bible, or at least to the memory of its
sound from their childhood. It has the beat and the
song of language that pleases the ear, and these
qualities are more than purely aesthetic considera-
tions. They represent a theological issue: the pastoral
need for language that suggests the depths of divine
personality through its tonal expressiveness.

The aural quality of language that gives witness to
God is an integral part of the total communication of
God's word. In fact, the conceptuality of our sermons
often makes a less lasting impact on the listener than
the sound in which the gospel is declared. Thus
David Grayson recalls of his childhood pastor: "Of
that preacher's sermons I remember not one word,
though I must have heard scores of them."[4]

But he can still hear the sound of the preacher's voice
when he would read from the Old Testament: "Those
splendid, marching passages, full of oriental imagery.
As he read there would creep into his voice a certain
resonance that lifted him and his calling suddenly above
his gray surroundings."[5] Although the preacher declared a gospel of gloom, the sound of his voice
triumphed over the dreariness of his thought so that
Grayson, in looking back over his childhood, is able to

say of that parson: "Heaven he gave me, unknowing, while he preached an ineffectual hell."[6]

Heaven was in the imagery and the cadence and the lift of the language. To acknowledge this is not to claim that the content of our sermons is unimportant. But it is to affirm that an essential aspect of the content is the aural quality of our language. To speak convincingly of a God who calls us to a life of faith and love requires a voice whose tonality is congruent with the personal character of the gospel we proclaim, and this is not possible if the sermon is delivered as a printed document that is being read to the congregation.

The Preacher's Voice as an Aural Symbol

In a sense, the voice of the preacher is an aural symbol, just as the chalice, the altar, and the cross are visual symbols. Paul Tillich has said that the best symbols erase themselves, that they draw us beyond what they are in themselves toward the ultimate reality that is their source, and this is precisely what good sermons do. The preacher's voice uses words and the physical properties of sound to draw people beyond the message that is being articulated into the presence of God. This is the reason that we cannot convey the power of a great sermon we have heard to someone else by repeating its content, and it is the reason why written sermons do not have the same impact as sermons delivered to a congregation.

Preachers, therefore, need to refine their capacity for the aural symbolization of the word of God, because it is the rhythm and tonality of speech that carry listeners "far below the conscious levels of thought and feeling, invigorating every word; sinking to the most primitive and forgotten, returning to the origin and bringing something back, seeking the beginning and the end.'"[7] It is from this primitive level of being that our deepest passions flow. Aural language engages those depths of human consciousness where we find the origins of cruelty and compassion, that place in the heart where we imagine our acts of violence and our acts of love.

The Rembrandt sermon employs such language in an attempt to transfuse the deepest levels of reality with the redemptive power of compassion. The sermon involves the congregation with the terror and suffering of violations of human rights by using the shorter evocative sentences of conversation to awaken their imaginative empathy for the victims:

> I call to the sleeping carpenter:
> "Wake up now."
> He does not stir.
> The boots stop.
> Silence.
> A baby cries down the street.
> Again silence.
> Then I hear a woman wailing.
> The boots begin again to mark their measured step.
> "Wake up, Joseph! For the love of God, wake up! Now."

No description that I could supply would be as vivid as what the listener's aroused imagination will create. The effect of the aural qualities of the speech is to invite the congregation into the reality so that they can respond out of the engagement of their compassion and sense of justice. This does not mean that sermons should never bring in statistics and hard data. Sometimes that material is crucial. But it is important that numbers and facts do not incapacitate the imaginative receptivity of the listeners.

Develop your sensitivity to the character of aural

communication by training your ear to listen as precisely as you are training your eye to observe and your body to feel. When you are in a public place—a restaurant, an airport, an athletic stadium, a theater before the concert begins—listen to the tones of people talking with each other. The content is not so important as the inflection and the color of speech. Notice how questions are often asked by simple sentences that are inflected with surprise.

"Who do you pick to win?"
"The rams by ten."
"The rams?"
"Yeah, the rams!"

Notice the repetition. Listen to the effect that is conveyed by the rise and fall of pitch, body posture, facial expression, the period of time between responses, the crescendo and decrescendo of the conversation as a whole. Language from the pulpit cannot be as informal as the conversation between two individuals because the preacher is trying to gather an entire community into an experience of the gospel, but effective sermonic speech will have the vivacity and drama that mark our everyday conversation and that make talking and listening to people fascinating.

Conveying Meaning by Sound

As in the case of expanding our visual and physical awareness, we are developing our aural sensibilities not simply as a dramatic technique but to be faithful to the whole truth of God. Vocal inflections represent dimensions of reality that exceed rational analysis, meanings that go beyond the denotations of a dictionary definition. Robert Frost referred to this phenomenon as "sound posturing":

> What we do get in life and miss so often in literature [and sermons!] is the sentence sounds that underlie the words.
>
> Words in themselves do not convey meaning, and to . . . (prove) this, which may seem entirely unreasonable to any one who does not understand the psychology of sound, let us take the example of two people who are talking on the other side of a closed door, whose voices can be heard but whose words cannot be distinguished. Even though the words do not carry, the sound of them does, and the listener can catch the meaning of the conversation. This is because every meaning has a particular sound-posture, or to put it in another way, the sense of every meaning has a particular sound which each individual is instinctively familiar with, and without at all being conscious of the exact words that are being used is able to understand the thought, idea or emotion that is being conveyed. What I am most interested in emphasizing in the application of this belief to art, is the sentence of sound, because to me a sentence is not interesting merely in conveying a meaning of words; it must do something more; *it must convey a meaning by sound.*[8]

Likewise, a sermon must convey a meaning by sound. I think, for example, of a sermon delivered to a group of preachers. It began by describing the various ways we feel trapped in life: by role, by circumstance, by self-doubt, by a constricted assessment of our gifts. During the early part of the sermon, the preacher's voice sounded like that of a person who was trapped. The meaning was conveyed by the sound of the voice as well as by the denotative meaning of the words.

Then the preacher moved into a transition about how the gospel springs us from the trap. The vocabulary turned from words of confinement to liberation, freedom, release, vision, and openness. But the congregation later revealed that they felt as trapped at the conclusion as they did at the beginning. I asked why, and someone answered: "The sound of the voice." The meaning conveyed by the sound had overridden the meaning conveyed by the words.

Getting sound and words to be congruent is a complex issue. Its resolution involves far more than adapting a "cheerier" tone of voice at the conclusion of the sermon. It requires a spiritual, theological process of finding that place in the heart where the gospel has touched the preacher's own life. Nothing can replace speaking out of that spiritual center. It is the place from which the melody of redemption arises and permeates our voice.

Listening to Our Own Music

If you can only create a sermon by writing it out, take time to read what you have written into a tape recorder and play it back to yourself without the manuscript before your eyes. How does it sound to you as a listener? Remember, this is the way your congregation will receive the sermon, not as readers but as listeners.

Plot the sermon on two graphs by content and tonality. In the sermon about being trapped, the two graphs would look like this:

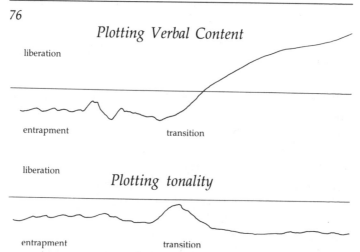

Are your graphs congruent, or is there a dissonance between the denotative meaning of the words and the sound posturing of the sermon? If there is dissonance, what is its source?

What do you need to do to make the content and the inflection sound in unison?

That work may involve prayer and spiritual reflection as well as rewriting.

If you have video equipment available, then you can also plot the nature of your gestures and your body posture. In the case of the sermon on being trapped, there was no increasing sense of physical freedom in the preacher's posture. The body remained as constricted as the voice, which reinforced the incongruency of the words and the tonality of the sermon.

The Sermon Manuscript as a Musical Score

Having tended to the spiritual and theological meanings revealed by the voice, you are now ready to consider other details about the aural character of your sermon. Does the language have the engaging music of good conversation? Are there long sentences that make fine sense to the eye on a page but perplex the ear? In the light of your listening, rework the manuscript the way you want to speak it.

Here is a sermon that I have laid out on the page to demonstrate what oral speech looks like. I do not always write a full manuscript, but in this case I did.

The pastor of the church in which I was the guest preacher had informed me that the parish had recently been through great controversy. He saw their next task to be reconciliation, not to gossip about one another, but to appreciate one another's gifts. I employed that intimate inflection that our voices take on when we gossip. I depended on the sound of the sermon almost as much as the content to bring the meaning home. The text, Mark 6:1-6, was assigned me from the lectionary.

A Sample Sermon

I can hear them now,
  the local gossips,
  trading the latest bits of scandal and hearsay—
whatever they have picked up
  from salespeople and pilgrims who have been
    passing through town.
I picture three of them
  sitting on a public bench, under a fig tree.
    Their major activity is
    enjoying the shade
      and fanning the air with their mouths.

One of them starts in:
"Did you hear what Mary and Joseph's son been doing
out round these parts?"
One of the gossips looks up, startled,
surprised but eager to be enlightened.
The other, with a tone of—"I know all about it"—declares:
"Yep, I heard.
Up to no good.
Been breaking Sabbath laws
and bringing disgrace on the home town.
Isn't that what you heard?"

"Well, kind of, but not exactly.
I heard things more amazing than that."
I picture the speaker, looking up through the branches
of the fig tree until he finds the ripest
fruit he can reach without having to stretch
too far.
He picks that single fig off the tree and takes one
small slow bite
while his friends sit there hungering
for his next sentence.
He wipes his lip and says in a perfectly calm voice:
"I hear he raised a dead girl."
"You're putting us on."
"Nope. I'm not. She's the daughter of a distinguished
Rabbi.
Jairus.
A member of his congregation told me the whole story.
Jairus was desperate.
His daughter was going fast.
He got on his knees
in front of a whole pack of people
and begged Jesus to come to his house.
Well,

Jesus started out,
    moving fast as he could with the crowd around him.
    Then all of a sudden,
    long before he gets to the house,
      he comes to a dead stop."
The speaker lifts the rest of the fig to his mouth
    and tells his friends—
    as though it is the very piece of news they are
waiting for—
    "You really ought to try one of these."
Then he takes a big breath and continues:
"A woman with a flow of blood
    saw him rushing by.
    Had no idea where he was headed.
      She reached out and touched his coat.
      And like that! she's healed.
Then he stood there praising her in front of everybody."

"See, I told you I knew all about it:
    Like I say:
    The man's out disgracing our town.
    Letting unclean women touch him,
    when he knows he's not supposed to act that way.
    I told you.
    I know his game."
    "I guess then you don't won't to hear the end of the
story."

The speaker surveyed the fig branches,
    as though he might eat the whole harvest
      before he finished his tale.

"Oh, go on and finish your story."

"Well, after the conversation with the woman,
    Jesus went on to the rabbi's house.
        But it was too late.
        The little girl was dead.
            The mourners were already there.
            But that didn't stop Jesus.
He sent them all out,
    took the child by her hand,
        and said clear as a bell to her:
        'Little Girl, get up.'
        And she got up and walked."

The speaker stops, and for a moment all you can hear
    is the wind in the fig tree,
        rustling through the leaves
        and sifting down the light
        of heaven's bright blue sky.

Then the gossip who has been quiet through the whole story,
    speaks up:
        "Are you talking about the same Mary and Joseph's son
        that I know?
        My neighbors down the street?
        She married real young,
            and he's a carpenter.
        They have some daughters who still live with them,
        and there are four other sons:
        James and Joses
            . . . and . . . and . . . give me a moment
            and I'll get their names
            . . . and Judas and Simon."
"Yep, that's the family.
    The oldest: Jesus.
    He's the one done all these things I told you about,

healed the woman with the flow of blood,
then raised the little girl from the dead.
And
  from all I hear
  that isn't half of it.
  That's just the most recent stuff."

The gossip who had claimed he knew it all,
  pulls down the first fig he can find
    and starts eating as though hunger has displaced
    any interest he might have in the story.

But the one who was quiet all this time
  begins to shake his head in skepticism.
    "It sure is hard to believe
    that your neighbor
      or your neighbor's child is a prophet.
  I remember when he was just a little tyke.
    I can picture him one day coming out
    of his father's shop.
    He had made himself a beard
    out of wood shavings
      and he was holding it up behind his ears.
  The thing kept falling down and unraveling.
    But he would pick it up and twine
    it together again.
  Once he got it all set, he started
    calling to his dad,
  'Abba, Abba, Abba,
    Come and see me.
    Come and see me.'
  And Joseph came out and picked him up in his arms,
    and the two of them laughed so hard
    you could hear it up and down the street.

It sure is hard to think of
  that laughing child grown to be a prophet."

"Well, I got one other piece of news then
  that may be of interest to you."
At these words, the sullen gossip
  stops chewing on figs and turns to listen.
"We're going to get a chance
  to see for ourselves
    if he's a prophet or not.
    I hear he's coming home,
    going to get to preach
    right here in his home synagogue."

"You'll see I was right
  once you hear him.
    He's done nothing but give this town a bad name
    in other places.
He's no prophet.
  How could he be?
Just use a little common sense.
  Would God, who made the heavens and the earth,
    show up in some neighborhood kid?"

"Wait a minute.
  I never said he was a prophet.
    I wasn't there to watch him raise the dead
    or heal that bleeding woman either.
All I told you was what I heard.
  I just pass on the news.
    I'm like both of you.
It doesn't make much sense to me
  to think God would work through
    a neighbor.

But I'm going to go hear him preach—
after all, I'm a little bit curious—
aren't you?"

I pick up the pulpit Bible and reread the gospel lesson, without any words of interruption, allowing the common speech of the sermon to be a frame around the picture that is painted by the familiar words of Scripture.

[Jesus] came to his own country; and his disciples followed him. And on the sabbath he began to teach in the synagogue; and many who heard him were astonished, saying, "Where did this man get all this? What is the wisdom given to him? What mighty works are wrought by his hands! Is not this the carpenter, the son of Mary and brother of James and Joses and Judas and Simon, and are not his sisters here with us?" And they took offense at him. And Jesus said to them, "A prophet is not without honor, except in his own country, and among his own kin, and in his own house." And he could do no mighty work there, except that he laid his hands upon a few sick people and healed them. And he marveled because of their unbelief. (Mark 6:1-6)

I place the Bible back on the pulpit and continue.

I can imagine
the gossip who lives down the street from Joseph and
Mary
a few days later
sitting alone on the bench
underneath the fig tree.
A traveling salesman,

whose business has led him to town,
 sits down on the same bench.
The salesman doesn't say anything right away
 because he can see that the gossip
 is lost in thought.
But the more the salesman studies his face,
 he sees that the man is distressed,
 and he is moved to ask:
 "Are you all right?"
The gossip turns his head
 and says to this perfect stranger
 what he might never say to his two friends
 who usually meet him at the fig tree:
 "No, not really.
 I'm upset.
 Sad about what happened last week
 in the synagogue."
The salesman looks puzzled
 and asks: "What was it?"
"Haven't you heard about this?
 People are talking about nothing else in this town.
 Where do you go to worship anyway?"
"Oh, it's a congregation far, far away from here.
 Meets in a beautiful building of my home city
 on Main and East. [The location of the congregation
hearing the sermon.]
 But what is it that happened here?"
And then the gossip tells the
 salesman the whole story
 of the neighborhood youngster
 who had grown up and
 made a name for himself out in the world
and then came home to be rejected by his own people.
When he finishes, the salesman reflects:

"Perhaps you all rejected him
   because you knew him from childhood.
   He was just one of you,
   like they say:
   'Familiarity breeds contempt.'
Or maybe people were jealous.
   You know how it is,
      they wish their child had done as well."
"No, I thought of all those things.
   But it was something deeper.
      There are two details you need to remember:
   First of all,
      when Jesus started speaking,
      everyone was impressed.
People were talking out loud in the service:
   'Where did this man get all this?'
   'What is the wisdom given to him?'
      I myself was moved.
      Even my two friends.
         They had tears in their eyes at one point,
            though they'd never admit it.
And then the other detail
   you need to remember is
      that Jesus did manage to heal a few people
      even after the rest of us turned against him.
I knew one of those he healed.
   I saw her face change when he touched her.
      Her eyes shone
      with a brightness
         I hadn't see in years.
But we discounted what we saw,
   and left, grumbling and disbelieving.
I can't shake the memory
   of how he moved us
      when he began to speak.

> And that woman he healed:
>> I see her shining eyes
>>> everywhere I go.
> No, it wasn't familiarity
>> and it wasn't jealousy.
> Through that woman's shining eyes
>> I see it was something more:
>>> In this young man
>>> God was coming closer to us
>>>> than God had ever been before.
>>> And we didn't want God to get that close.
> As long as God is only
>> the creator of the heavens and the earth,
>>> my friends and I can afford
>>> to sit on this bench
>>>> and talk about people
>>>>> any way we want to.
> Then on the sabbath,
>> we can thank God
>>> for the stars and the moon
>>> and the sun and the figs,
>>>> and return here the next day
>>>>> and take up our conversation
>>>>>> right where we left off.
> But if God
>> can approach us through
>>> our neighbor
>>> or our neighbor's child,
>>>> or our friend,
>>>>> or our wife or our husband
>>>>> or our colleague
> we can never again just take them for granted.
> If that is how God acts,
>> then we have to consider every single human being
>> a potential prophet,

a vessel of God,
a sign of holy love.
Do you have any idea
what that would do
to the conversations
that take place under this fig tree?"
A wind comes up
and sweeps the branches of the tree.
Some dark clouds are rolling
in off the Mediterranean
and it looks like rain is coming.
The two men fall silent,
until the Nazarene says to the salesman:
"And what about your congregation
back in your home town
at Main and East?"
Will they let God come close to them?
Can they see when God approaches them
through the young adult
whom they remember as a child, calling:
Mommy, Mommy, Mommy,
Daddy, Daddy, Daddy,
Come and see me.
Come and see me.
Can they see when God approaches them
over a cup of coffee with a friend
who is telling them the hard, but clear, truth
about their life?
Can they see when God approaches them
through the lifetime resident
who has surprised the whole neighborhood
with a petition for a just,
but unpopular, cause?
Can great wonders happen there
because they are open to God,

> who approaches them
>   through the most unlikely people?
> Or is your place like our Nazareth,
>   where Jesus "marveled
>   because of their disbelief"?
> A clap of thunder and the first patter
>   of rain on the fig leaves
>   sends the salesman running for his hotel
>   and the citizen of the town
>   dashing the other direction.
> As the salesman sits in his room
>   watching the rain,
>   his mind drifts to his home,
>   and he prays:
> "O God, who came to us in Jesus of Nazareth,
>   keep us open to your presence in each other,
>   that our risen savior will have no reason
>   to marvel because of our unbelief. Amen."

Notes

1. Plato, *Phaedrus.* In *Plato,* trans. H. N. Fowler, *The Loeb Classical Library Plato* (Cambridge, Mass.: Harvard University Press), p. 274. See also Hans-Ruedi Weber in *Experiments with Bible Study* (Philadelphia: The Westminster Press, 1981), p. 13. I am indebted to Weber's discussion of contemporary oral cultures for much of my argument in this section.

2. James Anderson Winn, *Unsuspected Eloquence: A History of the Relations Between Poetry and Music* (New Haven: Yale University Press, 1981), p. 17.

3. Lawrance Thompson and R. H. Winnick, *Robert Frost: A Biography* (New York: Holt, Rinehart and Winston, 1981), p. 172.

4. David Grayson, *Adventures in Contentment* (New York: Grosset & Dunlap, 1907), p. 124.

5. Ibid., p. 126.

6. Ibid., p. 131.

7. T. S. Eliot, quoted in Michael Edwards, *Towards a Christian Poetics* (Grand Rapids: William B. Eerdman's, 1984), p. 127.

8. Thompson and Winnick, *Robert Frost: a Biography,* pp. 210-11, emphasis added.

CHAPTER 5

*D*raw Parables from Life

When we are attentive to what we see, feel, and hear, our imaginations are less capricious and more reliable. The vividness of the world feeds our creativity day by day. We are less anxious about finding homiletical resources because we have become sensitive to the richness of common experience. We use our imaginations to draw parables from life, from plain human stories that are marked by ambiguity, resolution, and renewed ambiguity.

We prepare to leave home for school or our first job, and we find ourselves eager for freedom but wary of breaking with all that has nurtured us. Once we are gone, we discover that the world has more ambiguities than we ever imagined when we were back home.

We face surgery, glad that something can be done to correct our affliction, but frightened of the treatment itself. When we have made the last visit to the physician, who pronounces us well, we rediscover all the other ambiguities that were set aside while we struggled for health.

We start a project in our community, wondering if there will be any response. Relieved when people do respond, we become anxious for all the new ambiguities their interest awakens.

Looking for a Pattern

Throughout our lives we keep looking for a pattern, a meaning that flashes now and then into sight but finally keeps alluding us. We assume that our experience is parabolic, that it will illumine our ambiguities, that what has already happened holds the clue to what will happen or might happen or ought to happen if only we knew the right way to act.

When the preacher stands in the pulpit, we expect some light to be thrown on our quest. We do not necessarily ask that the sermon confirm all that we have been and done, although part of listening to a sermon includes a desire for such confirmation. Neither do we always seek a clear resolution to our ambiguities, for the more we experience life the more we are aware that life's resolutions are momentary and partial. But what we must have from the sermon is some "direction to the ambiguity,"[1] a sense that the convolutions of our lives form into some pattern of meaning.

"The Continuous Thread of Revelation"

Preachers cannot illumine the parabolic character of their listeners' lives if they have not understood the parabolic character of their own. To trace the parables of our lives is to find the revelatory connections of those events that hint of some purpose that eludes our usual perception. Eudora Welty explains how this process works:

> The events in our lives happen in a sequence in time, but in their significance to ourselves they find their own order, a timetable not necessarily—perhaps not possibly

—chronological. The time as we know it subjectively is often the chronology that stories and novels follow: it is the continuous thread of revelation.[2]

In finding the "continuous thread of revelation" we discover those experiential analogies by which our listeners can make sense of their own lives:

We understand one another, if at all, only through analogy. Who you are I know only by knowing what event, what focal meaning, you actually live by. And that I know only if I too have sensed some analogous guide in my own life. If we converse, it is likely we will both be changed as we focus upon the subject matter itself—the fundamental questions and the classical responses in our traditions. That analogical imagination seems and is a very small thing. And yet it does suffice.[3]

If our sermons lack such analogies, if they are devoid of parabolic resonance, then the preacher will fail to connect with the listener's systems of meaning because:

Anyone who would reason theologically must somehow succeed in mobilizing a shared awareness of the experiential grounds to which one's theological concepts appeal for their very meaning. Otherwise one's language, no matter how conceptual, is simply not understandable. In other words, only when a common standpoint of shared "religious" *experience* is established—and continually reestablished—can meaningful and sound reasoning using shared theological *concepts* be a real possibility.[4]

A Shared Awareness of Our Experience

The recent focus of homiletics upon narrative and imagery can be seen as nothing less than a corporate awakening in the church to the need for "mobilizing a shared awareness of the experiential grounds to which one's theological concepts appeal for their very meaning."

The descriptions of my study, the city of homiletical wisdom on my table, the skyline that I see out the dormer, the great silver maple tree that rises over my skylight—I have told you about these to encourage you to identify the experiential grounds of the sermons you create. What time and place are shaping your words as you give witness to God? What parables do they hold?

The Inspiration of Jesus' Parables

Jesus is my greatest inspiration for drawing parables from life. He did not create his parables from scratch. His stories reveal someone who is attentive to what is, who closely observes common human experience—the relationship of family members, the way people behave in the business world, the life of farmers and shepherds. It is striking how secular most of Jesus' parables are. There is almost nothing explicitly religious about them.

Learn from the Savior. Create parabolic stories or poems, depending on your natural bent as a writer, that have no blatantly religious tone or content but that reveal the truth and meaning of our lives in surprising ways. Save these pieces and periodically review them. You may then discover "the continuous thread of revelation" that would otherwise elude your most strenuous sermonic efforts.

A Sample of the Parabolic Process

Here is an example of the process that may make clearer what it means to trace the parabolic dimensions of common experience until they gather to a revelation.

Many years ago my wife received from her mother a plain black cupboard, about three feet high with a door made of a single plank that opens to three unevenly spaced shelves. The cupboard means a lot to the family because several generations ago a great uncle hammered it together from barnyard boards. His daughter, Rosalia, was going off to to teach at a boarding school, and she needed a modest storage cabinet to hold her belongings. It is the custom in my wife's family to keep such heirlooms and to pass them on to the children, along with the stories of the people who made and owned them. I have always found these stories fascinating and have been touched by the depth of meaning and feeling that these artifacts hold for my wife.

One day she decided to take the paint off the cupboard to see what kind of wood lay beneath all those coats of black. It turned out to be one of the most arduous refinishing projects she had ever undertaken. Yet, through the entire process her persistence had the character of a holy quest, as though in scraping off the paint my wife was peeling back time, returning to the long lost land where Rosalia had once lived.

I was so gripped by the intensity of my wife's engagement with the project that I found myself drawn into writing a poem. I had no thought of using the poem for a sermon or any other religious purpose. I simply knew that I needed to express the sense of wonder awakened by something so simple as scraping the black paint off an antique family chest.

A parable was happening before my eyes, a parable about my wife, her family and my delight in having been welcomed into the stories of their ancestors, a parable that awakened the following poem.

> I open the black cupboard door, a single wide warped
>   plank
> And from the shelved dark drifts the smell of sour
>   wood.
> I rub where the door rubbed before it shrank
> Then stand in the barn where I never stood
> And walk the farm I never walked
> Though I made many visits when Grandmother talked:
>
> "Two summers in a row the rain had drowned the crop
> And made in every field and yard a river, lake or pool.
> After which it rained some more, then still refused to
>   stop.
> So my sister had to take the offer from the boarding
>   school,
> Which wrote her back: 'For the attic dorm each teacher
>   brings
> A cupboard, wide as a single bed, to store her private
>   things.'
>
> Father gathered planks he'd laid to walk across the
>   muck.
> (Water stains and boot prints hide beneath those coats
>   of black.)
> 'If I had cash from beans,' he said, 'If I had better luck,
> I'd make no cupboard out of boards that when they dry
>   will crack.'

The wood kept drinking paint the way it had been
    drinking rain.
Once it downed the can, it still was showing grain.

Those rough unfinished spots Rosalia did not mind,
But the smell of barnyard boards she feared would fill
    the dorm.
She fixed up pomanders from cloves pressed into
    orange rind
To hide the heavy air of wood and earth and storm.
When all the crops were rotted, September came in fine,
And Rosalia rode to school with her cupboard made of
    pine."

The cupboard sits in my house now. I smell the flooded
    yard,
And I am glad for rains my family cursed,
That saved for me the things they would discard.
I rub the cupboard, tap the boards and thirst
To touch and see beneath the paint the wood they
    touched and saw,
To let my fingers read like Braille each crack and knot
    and flaw.

I brush on stripper, brace my weight against my putty
    knife
And scrape across the top. Black comes off revealing
    black.
I brush and scrape and brush and scrape as if there
    waited life
To be released by me. The paint first yields to my attack
A blade-wide strip of wood. I scrape some more and
    then I sand.
With every stroke I'm traveling back to see my family's
    land.

I place the cupboard in the hall where people leave their
    wraps.

Four coats of linseed oil have made the wood to glow.
Often as my guests come in they give it rubs and pats,
And when they put their coats back on they ask before
they go:
"Is that a family treasure?" Yes, I nod, then drift away
To field and farm and family the rain has turned to clay.

Two years after writing this personal parable, I was struggling to produce a hymn about doubting Thomas, John 20:19-31. I was having the same difficulties I have when exegesis and study have failed to stir in me a single idea for a sermon.

I went back through my files, looking at seemingly unrelated material that might reveal the "continuous thread of revelation" in my consciousness that would not have been evident when I first created the materials I was now reading. I came upon the poem about the cupboard and saw that it was concerned with far more than my wife's family. It was a parable about the need to touch, to see, to make visible and tangible the sources of our being.

I meditated on the line "To let my fingers read like Braille each crack and knot and flaw."

I read the gospel again. Doubting Thomas began to come into focus as my individual experience deepened toward its more universal human character through the consideration of the biblical text:

These things did Thomas count as real:
The warmth of blood, the chill of steel,
The grain of wood, the heft of stone,
The last frail twitch of flesh and bone.

The vision of his skeptic mind
Was keen enough to make him blind
To any unexpected act
Too large for his small world of fact.

His reasoned certainties denied
That one could live when one has died
Until his fingers read like Braille
The markings of the spear and nail.

May we, O God, by grace believe
And thus the risen Christ receive
Whose raw imprinted palms reached out
And beckoned Thomas from his doubt.[5]

The reflection on the earlier experience with the family cupboard had become the vessel of later revelation.

When we think about the parabolic nature of our lives in the light of God's Word, we find patterns of meaning larger than ourselves. We locate the thread of revelation that pulls us into the circle of the whole human family. And when we draw that thread of revelation into our sermons, then listeners begin to consider the parables of their own lives, and they become more attentive to where and how God is addressing them.

Notes

1. Eugene L. Lowry, *The Homiletical Plot: the Sermon as Narrative Art Form* (Atlanta: John Knox Press, 1980), p. 35.

2. Eudora Welty, *One Writer's Beginnings* (Cambridge, Mass.: Harvard University Press, 1984), pp. 68-69.

3. David Tracy, *The Analogical Imagination: Christian Theology and the Culture of Pluralism* (New York: Crossroad Publishing Company, 1981), pp. 454-55.

4. Burch Brown, *Transfiguration: Poetic Metaphor and the Languages of Religious Belief* (Chapel Hill: The University of North Carolina Press, 1983), pp. 164-65.

5. Carol Doran and Thomas H. Troeger, "These Things Did Thomas Count as Real." In *New Hymns for the Lectionary: To Glorify the Maker's Name* (New York: Oxford University Press, 1986), pp. 68-69.

CHAPTER 6

*U*nderstand the Church's Resistance to Imagination

Imagination is not always a welcome guest in the household of faith. Even preachers who say they want to become more creative often acknowledge discomfort about using their imaginations. Why is the pulpit ambivalent about using the imagination?

Is it because theology is supposed to deal with the truth, while imagination, at least in everyday speech, suggests fantasy, dreams, unreality? We dismiss illusions, saying, "It is all in your imagination." Is this why preachers resist the imagination at the same time that they desire its powers?

The True Illusion: Imagination and Reality as Opposites

I am in my study at dusk as I ask these questions, looking out my dormer window to the streets and the skyscrapers beyond my house. I notice in the distance a large American flag that is flying in the breeze on top of an apartment building. Someone is up on the roof, pulling the flag down in the evening light. It is too far away to make out the individual, but the slow pace of the flag's descent suggests that the person is lingering over the ritual.

I consider how that piece of red, white, and blue

cloth can awaken an enormous affective response in people. It is able to stir allegiance among the patriotic and to impress a system of order and authority on the imaginations of the citizens. Then I know why preachers must be concerned about the imagination: The socially constructed imagination of the city and the nation define the nature of our life together, shaping our ideas of what is fair and unfair and how we will respond to injustice and poverty.

Staring at that flag, I realize that the true illusion is not imagination itself, but setting imagination and the real world against each other. That dichotomy fails to recognize the constructive role of the imagination in defining what is real and unreal. Perhaps we discredit the imagination because it is too frightening for us to acknowledge how we depend on it for our definition of reality.

My eyes shift from the flag back to the homiletical city. I begin to gather from every neighborhood of the city of homiletical wisdom the books that may help me to understand the ambivalence that preachers feel about using imagination in the pulpit.

When we preachers resist something, we frequently seek the personal roots of our reaction. But there are occasions when our resistance is connected to something greater and more enduring than our private predilections. We are acknowledging a bias inherited from history and conveyed to us by the texture and tone of the community of faith that raised us or that supports us now.

I shove the tottering stacks of books I am not going to use to one end of the table and then begin rummaging through the volumes that I need, checking the handwritten indexes that I put in the back of nearly everything I read. Open books are spread next to open books, some of them overlapping to keep the stiff-backed ones from shutting closed on the passage that I want. I stand back for a moment and look at my homiletical city. I sense that the outward changes on the table are a symbol of the transfigurations in the heart that are brought about by opening ourselves to the imagination.

The Beginning of the History of Imagination

At first it is difficult to organize the material before me, but I discover that the difficulty is in the nature of the history of the topic.

> Until the Enlightenment we find nothing that could be called a fully worked out theory of imagination. Before that period we must piece together brief passages and even random remarks where the concept comes into play. As Harold Osborne has noted, there was no classical theory of what we today call "imagination," that is, of the capacity to mold experience, to bring something new out of the old or to sympathetically project oneself into the position of another.[1]

I reread the quotation and contrast the historic failure to articulate an understanding of the imagination with the development of classical rhetoric, which laid out the rules and principles of public speech and shaped the discipline of homiletics. I think of all the poetry, music, painting, sculpture, and architecture that the imagination of artists has created over the centuries to the glory of God. Why was there not "a fully worked out theory of imagination" to match the brilliant conceptualizations of rhetoric? Why was there instead what Mark Johnson calls "a deep prejudice against it in Western thinking?"[2]

We preachers are not the first to be puzzled by this question. In the late 1780s Johann Gottfried Herder wrote:

> Of all the powers of the human mind the imagination has been least explored, probably because it is the most difficult to explore . . . —it seems to be not only the basic and connecting link of all the finer mental powers, but in truth the knot that ties body and mind together.[3]

Thomas McFarland believes that people had not examined how the knot was tied because theological concepts explained the creativity of human beings, particularly belief in the soul and the transcendent dimensions of experience. But when the Enlightenment questioned these realities and lessened the assurance of faith, imagination emerged to bear the weight of the discredited theological formulations.

While I untangle these complex thoughts in my mind, I hear a wind rising in the crown of the great silver maple tree outside my skylight. The air is turning a heavier blue as dusk comes upon the city, and its tinge is reflected by the pure white walls of my study. I wonder how I will ever get all of these ideas together so that I can confidently draw upon the gifts of my imagination without violating my faith in Jesus Christ.

Since the Enlightenment is the historical turning point when people began to think more self-consciously about the principles and dynamics of the imagination, I will make a path of two kinds of books:

one on the left of the table will be books that were written prior to the Enlightenment, and those on the right will be books that were written after the Enlightenment. I begin to arrange the books, leaving the quotation by Herder at the center point where the two paths of books meet.

An ambulance goes by my dormer window, and its piercing wail snaps me out of the intensity of my intellectual pursuits. I realize how torn I am, as a preacher, between the immediacy of human need and the long-range perspective of human experience and thought that can keep my sermons from becoming merely faddish. If my full-time vocation were to be a professional historian, then I could amplify my references, checking out each nuance and turning of the human record. Or if I were called to tend only to the most urgent, crying needs of the human community, then I could abandon this struggle in my study. But, like all preachers, I am stretched between the two so that a more inclusive vision of human possibility and divine intention might emerge through my words.

I continue to arrange the books on my table. The last vapor of evening light hangs in the air as I finish putting them in order. I look up through the skylight at the tossing branches of the great silver maple. Words based on the first psalm rise from my heart: "Make me, God, like a tree planted beside the still water and not like the chaff that is carried away."

Imagination as a Subterranean Stream

As the wind blows in the tree, I picture again the statue of the two angels who appeared in the first chapter, the one with the trumpet and the other with the scroll. Out of the trumpet pours the sound of a great river. When the angels fade from sight, the roar of the river continues.

I listen. Now it sounds like a subterranean stream.

I look toward the homiletical city and the path of pre-Enlightenment books that begins at the city's edge. I remember the words "There is a river whose streams make glad the city of God."

What is this subterranean river whose source is heaven and that makes glad the city of homiletical wisdom? I pick up Augustine's *Confessions*, which earlier in the evening I had left open to the following passage, where he uses the word *memory* in a way that parallels the functions of the imagination:

> These acts I perform within myself in the vast court of my memory. Within it are present to me sky, earth, and sea. . . . There too I encounter myself and recall myself, and what, and when, and where I did some deed, and how I was affected when I did it. . . . From that same abundant stock, also, I combine one and another of the likenesses of things . . . and from them I meditate upon future actions, events, and hopes, and all these again as though they were actually present.[4]

Augustine's memory is far more than the simple recollection of former times and places. Memory does not strand him in the past but leads him to consider his future actions and what realities may yet come to be. Memory is for Augustine a world-creating faculty, visionary power, what we now term imagination.

I put down Augustine's words and trace my way farther along the path that leads from the homiletical city toward the Enlightenment, and as I proceed, the roar of the imagination becomes fainter. The river that the angel emptied out of heaven's trumpet has gone deeper underground. Although its waters are feeding the landscape above it, the inhabitants take its blessings for granted, and for century after century they seldom talk about how it feeds their creative energies. As Mark Johnson said, all we can find are "brief passages" and "random remarks" where the "concept comes into play."

A full moon has come up over my skylight. The branches of the great silver maple are sweeping across its face in rhythm to the wind, which groans through my study, filling it with a sense of energy and breath.

I would see better if I turned on the ceiling lights, but instead I settle for the gentlest lamp in the room. I do not want to disturb the inward balance of dream and reason by violating the outward balance of darkness and light. If I turned on the full wattage, I would provide you with a lucid step-by-step argument about the imagination. But I would be suspicious of such an account of the imagination because it would give no evidence that the imagination itself was feeding what was said. It would only be gossip about the imagination.

When I come to the Protestant Reformation it sounds as though the reformers are going to blast through the bedrock and drain the river dry. Although imagination itself is not the central subject of discussion, it is subsumed under the larger concerns of the corruption of humanity, and the judgment against imagination is severe. Martin Luther, in his commentary on Genesis 8:21, "The imagination of man's heart is evil from his youth," writes:

> We should therefore diligently study this passage since it so clearly shows that the nature of man is corrupt. The knowledge of man's natural corruption is most necessary, and it cannot be rightly understood without God's grace and mercy. It is a pity that this passage has been translated (in Latin) in such a way that it gave occasion to the sophists (the medieval teachers) to interpret it as though man's imagination were not itself evil but were only inclined to evil.[5]

John Calvin in a similar manner warns that the conceptions people hold of God

> are formed, not according to the representations he gives of himself, but by the inventions of their own presumptuous imaginations. This gulf being opened, whatever course they take they must be rushing forward to destruction. None of their subsequent attempts at the worship or service of God can be considered as rendered to him, because they worship not him but a figment of their own brains in his stead.[6]

As I read these quotations, the tape of television images moves in fast-forward through my head:

The dance to dishwasher detergent.
The pick-me-up bouquet.
The bodies in blood.
The touch down.
John 3:16.
The luxury car driving toward the beautiful mountain.
The high fiber cereal.

Martin Luther's and John Calvin's warnings about the imagination are not to be discounted. Watching television, in which the average length of shot is only 3.5 seconds, confirms the notion that when imagination is divorced from grace and truth, it is corruptible.

For a moment I am not able to hear the river that the angel poured out of heaven's trumpet. The only sound is the wind in the tree, and I look up through my skylight, wondering whether I must abandon the attempt to reconcile my vivid imagination and my passionate faith in Christ. Then I wander over to the other side of the room and look out the dormer toward the city and notice the flicker of light in an upstairs room, which indicates that the television is on. I think of how the city, indeed the entire country, is plugged into a corrupt, imaginative world, and that realization is enough to start me on my search again. If the power of God's grace is as magnificent as the Protestant reformers claimed, then grace can redeem even the corruptions of the human imagination.

I walk over to the table and reread the quotations of the reformers. Having recognized the truth of what they said, I now see their limitations as well. Neither Luther nor Calvin considers how his own imagination is engaged in the creation of his theology. There is none of the high self-consciousness about the role of the imagination that we find in a late twentieth-century theologian who writes a chapter entitled, "Christian Theology as Imaginative Construction," in which he observes:

> Theology is done by humans for human purposes; theological work must be assessed by human standards, and its judges are themselves always ordinary human beings. I mention these truisms because sometimes theologians have proceeded as though they

held in their hands superhuman divine truth, the Every Word or words of God.[7]

I read the quotation aloud and hear a protest immediately rising in the ancient sectors of the homiletical city. People are shouting:

What about revelation?
What about the transcendent truth of God?
What about the objectivity of the Word of God?
Do not give in to that stuff about Christian theology as imaginative construction.

But as I listen closely to the roar of their protest, what strikes me is that it sounds like the roar of the subterranean stream that the angel emptied out of heaven's trumpet! The objective, transcendent nature of God to which they give witness is revealed through the constructive work of their imaginations; one flows into the other as dream and reason, darkness and light, wind and stillness intermingle in my study.

Imagination Breaking to the Surface

I sit down at the table and read how the Enlightenment loosened the encapsulating assumptions of Christian thought. The underground stream of the imagination broke to the surface, and philosophers and poets began to study and celebrate its role in creating our perception of the world.

There was an enormous acceleration, beginning in the late seventeenth and early eighteenth centuries, of the sense of imagination's importance . . . imagination became so important because soul had been so important and because soul could no longer carry its burden of significance. That significance was an assurance that there was meaning in life. No soul, no meaning. But even if soul wilted under the onslaught of science and skepticism, so long as there was imagination as secondary validator then at least there remained the possibility of meaning.[8]

I scan the quotations I read earlier in the evening, which follow after this central turning point in the Enlightenment. I want to have some sense of where this mighty river that has broken to the surface will carry us. I go to the farthest end of the path of books that leads from the Enlightenment. I have had to place the last few volumes on the counter because I ran out of room on the table. I walk over to the counter and read the observation of twentieth-century poet Wallace Stevens: "One of the visible movements of the modern imagination is the movement away from the idea of God."[9] I hear a chorus from certain sections of the homiletical city, crying in unison: "We warned you."

I discover that after imagination emerged as a central faculty of human thought and meaning, there were believers who attacked its dangers, while others claimed its importance for Christian theology.

Jonathan Edwards, for example, develops the role of imagination in addressing a gap in John Locke's epistemology—namely, how to explain the mind's orderly experiencing of reality when it depends on sense impressions. Edwards came to acknowledge that "the true character of God" is known through our "imaginative perception," which supplies something that our "discursive or conceptual reason cannot know."[10]

As the moonlight fills my study and I feel in my body the exhilaration and exhaustion of this night's struggles, I sense the truth of Edwards's insight. I wonder whether in some ways his work might represent an early instance of homiletics as the discipline of imaginative theology.

I get a glass of water, and the coolness at my lips brings back the memory of champagne and the mother of the bride, whose divorced relatives had been so thankful for my wedding sermon. I find my eyes filling with tears at the sheer joy of being a preacher, to be called to speak words that touched a family so deeply, and then afterwards to lay out all these books and try to understand that simple human act of ministry in the light of an entire tradition and history. My heart overflows with prayer for the couple who were married and the mother of the bride and her sister and cousin and their children and the historical figures who produced the books that lie on the table in the moonlight.

As I sit down and consider the lateness of the hour, the path of books that leads from the Enlightenment, and my alternating states of prayer and study, I wonder whether I am going a little mad. Then I remember the Christian poet Christopher Smart, who lived from 1722 to 1771, the very period when the subterranean river of imagination was breaking to the surface. Smart got caught in the current, and his peers judged him to be crazy. They locked him up in an asylum because he would fall on his knees at street corners and implore people to pray with him.

I once preached a sermon about Smart that illustrates the themes of this chapter. Below is a condensed version of the sermon, illustrating the kind of madness we have to risk if we are going to preach the gospel.

A Sample Sermon

My sermon topic this morning is "The Great Flabber Dabber Flat Clapping Fish with Hands." That is a line from the poem, "Rejoice in the Lamb" by the eighteenth-century poet Christopher Smart. Portions of his poem have been set to music by Benjamin Britten in a popular cantata that is often featured in sacred choral concerts.

Christopher Smart's contemporaries could not understand his imagination. It was the Age of Reason. Where was the evidence of reason in someone who wrote "The great flabber dabber flat clapping fish with hands"?

The scholarship of a later time would show that crazy Christopher was not so crazy after all. At the end of his flabber dabber line, he wrote a note telling people to look up Anson's Voyage *and Psalm 98.* Anson's Voyage *was a popular work of natural history, which featured among its illustrations flat fish jumping out of the water and seals with fins like hands. Psalm 98, verse 8 reads: "Let the floods clap their hands."*

Flabber dabber is the sound of a seal clapping its fins.

Flabber dabber is the sound of the floods clapping their hands.

Flabber dabber is the compressed insight of a great imaginative poet using his creative powers to combine the scientist's observation and the psalmist's praise. Flabber dabber represents a vision of one unified world of science and faith, rationality and imagination. Flabber dabber reveals a mind far in advance of its own time, already working on great issues that would consume the energies of philosophers and theologians and common people as the

Christian faith tried to come to terms with the discoveries of Darwin and the impact of industrialism.

But the constricted rationalism of his own age did not allow for the visionary powers of Christopher Smart. The church lacked the imagination that would make it possible to see that Christopher was more faithful than he was crazy.

The story of Christopher Smart brings to mind other people who sounded like flabber dabber to those who heard them. I think of a Nazarene carpenter going about the countryside, preaching that the kingdom of God is at hand. People responded, "He is beside himself." It sounded like flabber dabber to them.

I think of the women running back from the tomb and saying "He is risen" and the disciples dismissing their words as nothing more than an "idle tale." It sounded like flabber dabber to them.

When Paul proclaimed the gospel and spoke of the cross, it was "a stumbling block to Jews and folly to Gentiles." It sounded like flabber dabber to them.

Who is speaking flabber dabber now? Is it those who announce that the nations of the world could live in peace and you and I can help bring it about? Is it those who say that even in a strained economy we can provide adequate medical care, food, and shelter for all of our citizens? Is it the friend who believes deeply enough in you to hold up a vision of how you could break some destructive pattern of behavior?

When you hear what sounds like flabber dabber, do not simply dismiss it as madness. For it may be divine madness, the madness of One who conceived a billion, billion stars, and a planet blue and green, and a Savior rising from the grave.[11]

Claiming Imagination for the Church

When the imagination emerged as a topic and theme of public discourse at the end of the

Enlightenment, it sounded like flabber dabber to many good church people. However, some theologians and preachers, tried to claim the imagination for the purposes of faith and the witness of the church.

One of them was Friedrich Schleiermacher, who in 1800, reacting against the high rationalism of his German contemporaries, praised "this divine power of the imagination, which alone can free the spirit and place it far beyond coercion and limitation of any kind, and without which man's sphere is so narrow and precarious!"[12]

I put down Schleiermacher's book and consider how "narrow and precarious" my world would be without the imagination—looking at the moon and seeing nothing but a satellite 250,000 miles away; looking at the maple tree and seeing nothing but its bare branches; looking at the city and seeing nothing but buildings of steel and concrete; looking at my table and seeing nothing but piles of books; looking at a biblical text and seeing nothing but the denotative meaning of its words. Then I realize that imagination is inescapable. It takes imagination to imagine the world without imagination. Our politics, our response to suffering, our receptivity to beauty, our belief and unbelief—all of these involve how we imagine the world.

Do we imagine it to be bare and desolate and without witness to any redeeming power?

Do we imagine it as nothing more than the supplied images of the age in which we live:

the dance to dishwasher detergent;
the pick-me-up bouquet;
the luxury car driving toward the beautfiful mountain?

Or do we imagine the world through what Samuel Taylor Coleridge calls "the primary imagination," defining it as "the living Power and prime Agent of all human Perception, and as a repetition in the finite mind of the eternal act of creation in the infinite I AM?"[13] This is imagination that draws its energies from the source and sustainer of our lives, the One to whom we give witness.

"The God-Power in the Soul"

It appears that Henry Ward Beecher had some idea of this process. In his famous *Yale Lectures on Preaching* (1872–1874) he named imagination the most important prerequisite for effective preaching. He used a phrase that is strikingly similar to Coleridge, calling it "the God-power in the soul" by which he means "the power of conceiving as definite the things which are invisible to the senses,—of giving them distinct shape."[14]

This night in my study, I have been trying to record what the exercise of "the God-power in the soul" involves. It is a rhapsodic, rational, prayerful, thoughtful, all-embracing process that replicates through the limitations of human language and action the pulsations of the heart of reality.

Through the God-power in the soul, we hear our Creator playing what Christopher Smart calls "the harp of stupendous magnitude and melody./For at that time malignity ceases and the devils themselves are at peace." The music from "the harp of stupendous magnitude and melody" is one with the music of the angel's trumpet that poured out the streams that are feeding the homiletical city and are circling around and through my study.

I look up from my books and find the "God-power in my soul" surrendering to the ache in my back and the soreness of my eyes. I can hear Paul the apostle telling me, "We have this treasure in earthen vessels in order to show that the transcendent power belongs to God and not to us." I stand up to stretch my back and think "earthen vessel." I rub my eyes and think "earthen vessel." I sit back down and read the electronic noodle alphabet that records this chapter and think "earthen vessel, earthen vessel."

The Fear of Madness and Sensuality

Then I turn to my books and scan from quotation to quotation about the risks of the imagination. I read of how the imagination was associated with the constricted world of private fantasy and even madness. No less a figure than Samuel Johnson, who was gracious enough to befriend Christopher Smart, considered this faculty of the mind to be

> related to sin and sensuality, to emotional instability and madness. It was related directly to all those ills of the body and the soul that kept man from reflecting on his true concerns, namely, his quest for salvation. Johnson made this more general point explicit in a prayer he wrote on March 31, 1771. "O Lord God, in whose hand are the wills and affections of man, kindle in my mind holy desires, and repress sinful and corrupt imaginations. Enable me to love thy commandments, and to desire thy promises; let me by thy protection and influence so pass through things temporal, as finally not to lose the things eternal." And thus the imagina-

tion became for Johnson not only the enemy of reason but the antagonist of faith.[15]

"The enemy of reason" and "the antagonist of faith"—neither phrase describes my experience of imagination. The imaginative work of this night has not been the enemy of reason. In fact, it has flowed from many months of reading and rational thought. The way I organized the books on my table was an act of logic that facilitated the poetic vision of the stream. And all that I have seen and felt by the grace of imagination has deepened, strengthened, and expanded my faith.

Yet, I know how persistent Johnson's view of the imagination is. A century later, when Beecher delivered his lectures and praised the imagination, he acknowledged: "In godly families it was, formerly, the habit to discourage the imagination, or to use it only occasionally. They misconceived its glorious functions."[16]

It probably sounded like flabber dabber to them.

"Hallelujah from the Heart of God"

As I go to turn off the computer, I recall another line from Christopher Smart's poem: "Hallelujah from the heart of God." Notice that Smart says hallelujah *from* the heart of God, not *to* the heart of God. There is great theological insight here. When we praise God—and *hallelujah* means "Praise the Lord"—whether it be through prayer or sermon or action, we are not initiating some action on our own. Rather we are tuning ourselves to an action that God has already started. Our hallelujah continues the hallelujah from the heart of God. The sermons we preach become an extension of God's own initiating action. Our words stir others to praise because they echo the praise that fills the universe.

Notes

1. Mark Johnson, *The Body in the Mind: The Bodily Basis of Meaning, Imagination, and Reason* (Chicago: The University of Chicago Press, 1987), p. 141.

2. Ibid., p. 140.

3. Quoted by Thomas McFarland, *Originality and Imagination* (Baltimore: The Johns Hopkins University Press, 1985), p. xiii.

4. Augustine, *The Confessions of St. Augustine*, trans. John K. Ryan (New York: Doubleday/Image Books, 1960), Book 10, chapter 8 (14), pp. 237-38.

5. Martin Luther, *Luther's Commentary on Genesis*, trans. J. Theodore Mueller (Grand Rapids: Zondervan Publishing House, 1958), p. 159.

6. John Calvin, *On the Christian Faith: Selections from the Institutes, Commentaries, and Tracts*, ed. John T. McNeill (Indianapolis: Bobbs-Merrill Company, Inc., 1957), p. 11.

7. Gordon D. Kaufman, *The Theological Imagination: Constructing the Concept of God* (Philadelphia: The Westminster Press, 1981), p. 263.

8. McFarland, *Originality and Imagination*, p. 151.

9. Milton J. Bates, *Wallace Stevens: A Mythology of Self* (Berkeley: University of California Press, 1985), p. 212.

10. Sang H. Lee, "Imagination and the Increasing Reality in Jonathan Edwards." In *Pre-Printed Paters for the Section on Philosophy of Religion and Theology*, compiled by David Griffin for the American Academy of Religion Annual Meeting, 1973, p. 39.

11. I first preached this sermon in a worship service that featured our chapel choir singing selections from Britten's musical setting of "Rejoice in the Lamb." The exposition of "flabber dabber" helped the congregation to broaden its receptivity to the poetry and the music so that the listeners' imaginations were opened to a deepened experience of the Holy Spirit. The unified expression of word and music or other liturgical art is often one of the most effective ways of reducing resistance to the imagination in worship.

12. Friedrich Schleiermacher, *Schleiermacher's Soliloquies*, trans. Horace Leland Friess (Chicago: The Open Court Publishing Company, 1926), p. 81.

13. Samuel Taylor Coleridge, *Biographia Literaria*. In *The Collected Works of Samuel Taylor Coleridge*, ed. James Engell and W. Jackson Bate (Princeton: Princeton University Press, 1983), vol. 7:1, p. 304. See footnote 4 on pp. 304-05 of this reference for a list of the English and German thinkers on whom Coleridge is drawing.

14. Henry Ward Beecher, *Yale Lectures on Preaching* (New York: Fords, Howard, & Hulbert, 1896), pp. 110-11.

15. Charles Pierce, Jr., *The Religious Life of Samuel Johnson* (Hamden, Conn.: The Shoe String Press, Inc., 1983), pp. 59-60.

16. Beecher, *Yale Lectures on Preaching*, p. 109.

CHAPTER 7

Dream of New Worlds

Last week I had some visitors to my attic study. Walking upstairs into the room, one of them blurted out: "Look at these books all over the place!"

I explained, "I am in the middle of writing a book."

"How can you find anything? You ought to have those books in shelves, organized by author or category."

Today I am in my study alone, smiling at the memory of the visitor. The table stacked with books appears alternately as a mess that needs to be picked up and a city of wisdom with a river flowing from it. The oscillation of perspectives reminds me of how different the world appears to various individuals and groups.

"Metaphors We Live By"

We spend our childhood in mastering the imaginative conventions of the communities that raise us: what is good and what is bad, what is right and what is wrong. Through speech and ritual, we are introduced to the politics of imagination, to the relative power of the various metaphors that guide the community's perception and behavior. Because these constitute our native tongue, they are second nature to us and we do not question their peculiarities the way we do a foreign language. We assume that the world is the way we speak it, that reality matches the "metaphors we live by." The phrase is from George Lakoff and Mark Johnson, who have studied the fundamental figurative patterns of speech in our society: "We have found . . . that metaphor is pervasive in everyday life, not just in language but in thought and action. Our ordinary conceptual system, in terms of which we both think and act, is fundamentally metaphorical in nature."[1] When we grow up, it is easy to assume that the way we were taught to imagine the world is the way the world is, or at least the way it is supposed to be.

Training our attentiveness to what we see, feel, and hear can awaken a fresh imagining of reality, stirring dreams and visions of a new creation in which the gospel is embodied in daily life.

Postmodern Preaching and the Suspicion of Authority

Before we can preach those sacred visions effectively, we need to understand how our listeners imagine the world. They do not live in biblical times or reformation times or even modern times. They live in the postmodern, mass media age that has conditioned them to perceive and experience the world in new ways.

We can gain a strong sense of the difference between modern and postmodern preaching by turning to Harry Emerson Fosdick's *The Modern Use of the Bible*. When Fosdick was preaching, the word *modern* was a loaded term, filled with the controversies that had been set off by the scientific revolution, particularly by Darwinism, and the development of historical biblical studies:

> When one moves back to the Scripture with a mind accustomed to work in modern ways, he finds himself in a strange world. The people who walk through its pages often do not speak his language, nor use his intellectual viewpoints, nor explain occurrences by his categories. . . .
>
> Here is the perplexity which more than any other afflicts the minds of educated men. They honor the Bible. They know that in it are the springs of the noblest elements in our civilization. They stand uncovered before Jesus Christ. But they are honestly bothered by many things in Scripture. They do not know what to make of them[2]

I am struck by how much authority *both* Scripture and science carry for Fosdick. He often appeals to "modern astronomy," "modern biology," "modern physics" and "modern medicine." As I read his words, I replay in my mind a number of recent newscasts about ecological and medical disasters:

> A swamp in Louisiana that used to be a refuge for birds and fish is now dead from the seepage of petroleum distillates.
>
> Computer generated pictures of the growing hole in the earth's ozone layer.
>
> Trees dying from acid rain in Vermont.
>
> A defeated looking physician in a wrinkled white coat, standing before a forest of microphones and disputing a court decision about medical ethics case.

When the replays finish running in my brain, I turn back to the city of homiletical wisdom, and I discover that the authority of Scripture has become as questionable as the authority of modern science and technology. Fosdick could expect his audience to concur when he observed that "in [the Bible] are the springs of the noblest elements in our civilization." But that truth is no longer self-evident in the city that has arisen on my table.

My eye wanders to the postmodern neighborhood, where I catch sight of *Texts of Terror: Literary-Feminist Readings of Biblical Narratives,* in which Phyllis Trible removes the possibility of hiding the horrors of our scriptural tradition behind a facile apologetic. Instead of the modernist quest, seeking to reconcile the authority of Scripture with the authority of science, the assumption of authority is laid aside, and we consider the suffering of women in the Bible, whose "passion has its own integrity."[3]

We might summarize our discoveries this way: Modern preaching sought to bring recognized authorities into harmony with each other, while postmodern preaching works under the suspicion of all authority that now pervades our culture. One of the reasons we must alert our eyes to keener sight and feel the bodily weight of truth is that if we do not ground our sermons in the actuality of experience, the authority of what we say will be suspect. Appeals to the Bible or tradition do not carry sufficient weight in themselves.

A Proliferation of Hermeneutics

Fosdick was rapturous about the historical-critical method of biblical criticism and what it portended for preaching. He exclaimed:

The world in which the Bible first was written lives again in our thought. We can enter into its mind, understand its problems, catch the native connotations of its words. Historic imagination has well accredited data on which to work and can picture how men [and women] lived, thought, talked, and hoped in Scriptural times. Perhaps what has been gained is as nothing in comparison with the light that yet shall come but, for all that, it is true that when we read the Book to-day we read it with increasing clearness in terms of its contemporary meanings. In a way never true in Christian history before we stand face to face with the historic sense of the Scriptures.[4]

But now in our own time there is a proliferation of hermeneutics, and some of our most distinguished literary critics question the cumulative result of historical criticism. Northrup Frye, reflecting on his efforts to teach the Scriptures to non-theologically trained students, discovered:

The analytical and historical approach that has dominated Biblical criticism for over a century was of relatively little use to me, however incidentally I may depend on it. At no point does it throw any real light on how or why a poet might read the Bible. I have suggested elsewhere that textual scholarship has never really developed the "higher" criticism that made such a noise in the nineteenth century. Instead of emerging from lower criticism, or textual study, most of it dug itself into a still lower, or subbasement, criticism in which disintegrating the text became an end in itself. As a result its essential discoveries were made quite early, and were followed by a good deal of straw-thrashing.[5]

Frye's critique represents a loss of authority from within the community of Western literary critical discourse. But even more challenging are the perspectives of Third World and feminist theologies, which question the privileged position of Western male hermeneutics. Next to Northrup Frye, I find several other postmodern books, including Robert McAfee Brown's disturbing volume *Unexpected News*, in which I read:

> Third world Christians think that people like us read the Bible from the vantage point of our privilege and comfort and screen out those parts that threaten us. They tell us that the basic viewpoint of the biblical writers is that of victims, those who have been cruelly used by society, the poor and oppressed. They further tell us that they are the contemporary counterparts of those biblical victims, cruelly used by contemporary society, the poor and oppressed.[6]

Where Do We Stand When We Look?

The subtitle of Brown's book is "Reading the Bible with Third World Eyes"—the word *eyes* is significant because it emphasizes how we see the Bible, how we see the world, how our understandings are shaped by where we stand in the systems of political and social power. Seeing is as much an act of the imagination as it is the eye, and Brown persistently asks us what factors of self-interest have determined the focus of our imaginations.

New Eyes for Reading: Biblical and Theological Reflections by Women from the Third World, a recent collection of biblical and theological reflections by women from the Third World, reveals this same concern for our perceptual bias. I thumb through the pages until I find a story that has haunted me since I first read it because it challenges the metaphors we live by and reveals the dangers of the imaginative conventions we take for granted.

In her meditation "One Woman's Confession of Faith," Lee Oo Chung, president of the Korean Women Theologians Association, tells of an ancient bell that was famous for its beautiful tone. It had been commissioned by a king as a way of showing the people's devotion to Buddha. The king's advisors had told him that making a huge temple bell would secure the nation from foreign invasion. The specialist who cast the bell had produced several failures until he concluded that the best way to produce a great bell was to sacrifice a young maiden:

> Soldiers were sent to find and fetch such a young girl. Coming upon a poor mother in a farm village with her small daughter, they took the child away, while she cried out piteously: *"Emille, Emille!"*—"Mother! O Mother!" When the molten lead and iron were prepared, the little girl was thrown in. At last the bell maker succeeded. The bell, called the Emille Bell, made a sound more beautiful than any other.
>
> When it rang, most people praised the art that had produced such a beautiful sound. But whenever the mother whose child had been sacrificed heard it, her heart broke anew. Her neighbors, who knew of her sacrifice and pain, could not hear the beautiful tone without pain either.
>
> Only those who understand the sacrifice can feel the pain. Others just enjoy the sound.[7]

I put down the book with the story of the bell on top of a book about the Enlightenment. I begin to imagine the tolling of our seminary bells, which hang in the great tower that dominates our Neogothic buildings. I delight in the deep resonant bong of those bells. Someone in our neighborhood recently wrote the city newspaper to express her thanks for the music they play each day. But now I listen to them with the ears of Lee Oo Chung and realize:

> The beauty of the sound of the bells
>   rings from a tower
>   that rises from a building
>   that houses a school
>   that teaches a tradition
>   that grows from a history
>   that flows with the blood
>   of slaves who were chained
>   and women who were silenced
>   as the church gave witness
>   to Christ who inspired
>   the people who built
>   the tower that rings
> with the beauty of the sound of the bells.

I look at the homiletical city and imagine the slow tolling of a single resonant bell as I reread Lee Oo Chung's words, "Only those who understand the sacrifice can feel the pain. Others just enjoy the sound." Her words and the sound of the bell sweep over the homiletical city, and I begin to consider how everything before me, all my treasured books, the river of imagination, even the visions that have inspired me in the nighttime hours arise from a history that fuses together beauty and brutality as inseparably as the flesh of the little girl and the lead and iron of the bell.

Claiming the Beauty and the Terror of Our Past

The congregation that led me to faith introduced me to that ambiguous history. I remember the church of my youth with affection. Visitors used to say of the white clapboard high steepled structure, "It looks right out of Currier and Ives."

What did your childhood church look like? What did the choir sing? What do you remember that you still treasure? These early impressions often exercise a powerful, but unacknowledged, influence over preachers.

While the bell continues to toll in my mind, I picture entering the sanctuary with my mother and turning left to the pew where we always sat. It gave us a good view of the high raised dark wood pulpit and the American flag that jutted out from the frame of the stain-glassed window of Easter lilies.

Despite years of study and teaching in a pluralistic seminary, there are few things that more immediately mobilize my affective sense of the wonder of God than singing particular hymns or hearing certain passages of Scripture that were repeated again and again in that church. I can still sense the other members of the congregation sitting around us, and I can pick out certain voices as we sing the hymns. We had all come together because in our own stumbling way we loved Jesus and we wanted to serve him. There we were, sitting still as stones during the sermon, then singing our lungs out on a favorite hymn:

Guide me, O thou great Jehovah,
Pilgrim through this barren land.
I am weak, but thou art mighty;

> Hold me with thy powerful hand.
> Bread of heaven, bread of heaven,
> Feed me till I want no more;
> Feed me till I want no more.

When I sit in my study and the moon shines on the homiletical city and the wind blows in the tree and I offer up prayers shaped by the psalms and the words of Jesus, I am feeding on the bread of heaven. I am drawing on the faith that those childhood worship services planted and nurtured in me. I am employing the metaphors I live by, the conventional religious imagination of the congregation that led me to Christ. The tree and moon are melded with the biblical images because when we came out of youth fellowship meetings on Sunday evenings, after singing "Follow, Follow the Gleam" we often looked up through the maple trees and remarked about the moon or the stars. Scripture, nature, and hymnody were one seamless piece of consciousness in my most formative church experience, and my later theological reading about the distinctions between natural and revealed theology, no matter how rationally persuasive, never convinced my heart.

But now the tolling of the Emille Bell and the remembrance of my past blend into a single reverberation. I begin to consider the fusion of beauty and pain that was alive in the church that raised me and that gave me the faith I proclaim as a preacher.

Surely there was beauty in that church, not only the aesthetic beauty of the music and the eloquence of our pastor's preaching, but moral and intellectual beauty as well. There was the beauty of courage in the face of fatal disease, the beauty of compassion for people in need, and the beauty of a faith that combined thought and feeling, a faith that has brought me through sorrow, given me a modicum of grace, provided courage to stand for justice, saved me from insanity, taught me that I was a person of worth, made me a member of the community, and led me to know that Jesus is my Savior and friend.

But like the Emille bell, and like the bells in the seminary tower, this beauty was mixed with injustice and tragic sacrifice. I recall a particular service when, as a young teenager, I sensed for the first time the frightful underside of the community of faith.

It was summer, sometime in the late 1950s, as Martin Luther King, Jr., received increasing news coverage for his desegregation efforts. Our upstate New York town was entirely white. We seldom saw black people. There were few, if any, migrant workers in the surrounding countryside because most of the farms were small family dairies. But our pastor felt moved by the Spirit to speak out in favor of what King was trying to do and to remind us as a congregation that we had a Christian obligation to support full civil rights for all people. I remember going to the coffee hour afterwards and hearing someone viciously attack the sermon: "I don't see what it has to do with the gospel or with our lives. Everything seemed fine until this troublemaker stirred them up."

In reporting this, I do not mean to sound as though I understood what the sermon had to do with our lives. I cannot recall any particular reaction that I had except surprise at the amount of acrimony in the coffee hour. But now, some thirty years later, with equality for all still a dream, I see the limitations of the religious imagination of the congregation that raised me. I hear not only the beautiful sound of the bell but also the pain, the unspeakable pain of generations of black people and the terror of racism that was fused with the imaginative vision of the faith whose beauty has sustained me.

I travel from my childhood church back to the homiletical city and consider the neighborhoods that were built prior to the rise of feminism and the opening of Western consciousness to black and Third World theologies. The academic theological and philosophical world is no less a mixture of truth and distortion. There are enduring values in those older neighborhoods, but when I consider them in the light of the expansions of the last three decades, I can see that they are theological ghettos, regions of constricted imagination whose limitations do not become fully apparent until I turn to the postmodern buildings.

Correcting the Distortions of Faith

How will the city of homiletical wisdom settle the political battles of imaginative theology? Will we look back at the limitations of the old theological structures and decide that they are such amalgamations of pain and beauty, injustice and gospel that they must now be abandoned for what is totally new?

I think again of the church of my childhood. My heart fills simultaneously with thanksgiving and sorrow: thanksgiving for the people who had the faith to pass on the faith that their parents passed on to them, sorrow for all the tragic failures and distortions of that faith.

Slow as a cloud drifting behind the branches of the

great silver maple tree, a revelation moves across the
landscape of my heart. I am beginning to realize
  it is the truth of faith
    that gives me the faith
      to follow the Spirit by faith
        in correcting the distortions of faith.
The same pattern of transformation can help
preachers to dream of new worlds and to create
sermons for our postmodern age. Rosemary Radford
Reuther describes this as a process in which "we
appropriate the past not to remain in its limits, but to
point to new futures."[8]

Postmodern preachers draw on the past not to give
listeners that old time religion but to demonstrate
"the critical principle that Biblical faith applies to
itself." The principle involves removing "the ideo-
logical mystifications that have developed in the
tradition of Biblical interpretation and that have
concealed the liberating content. The prophetic
advocacy of the poor and the oppressed and the
denunication of unjust social hierarchies and their
religious justification leap into clear focus."[9]

Postmodern preachers model to their listeners that
they can

  draw on the truth of faith
    to receive the faith
      to follow the Spirit by faith
        in correcting the distortions of faith.

A Vision Comes to the Preacher

Faith is correcting faith while I work in my study.
The river that flowed through the city of homiletical
wisdom during the night hours returns. But this time

the river and the city have changed in appearance. I see neighborhoods that were never there before. I have always imagined the city in my study to be like the city of skyscrapers and wood frame residences that is outside my window, but now I see huts and shanties. Where I traced the course of a single river that started underground and then broke to the surface at the time of the Enlightenment, I now see dozens of rivers.

The multiplication of waterways calls to mind Langston Hughes' great poem "The Negro Speaks of Rivers." I go to my bookcase to find a copy. It is not in the city of homiletical wisdom. The selectivity of what I placed there reveals that my own imaginative work has been too narrow. I had made room in the city for Christopher Smart, a white poet, but not for the black poet, Langston Hughes. The imagination of my childhood faith has been constricting my vision at the same time that it has been fueling my efforts to expand the imaginative range of preachers.

I find Langston Hughes in the bookcase and read his poem aloud to all the citizens of the homiletical city, but above all to myself:

> I've known rivers:
> I've known rivers ancient as the world and older than the flow
>   of human blood in human veins.
>
> My soul has grown deep like the rivers.
>
> I bathed in the Euphrates when dawns were young.
> I built my hut near the Congo and it lulled me to sleep.
> I looked upon the Nile and raised the pyramids above it.
> I heard the singing of the Mississippi when Abe Lincoln went

down to New Orleans, and I've seen its muddy
bosom turn
   all golden in the sunset.

I've known rivers:
Ancient, dusky rivers.

My soul has grown deep like the rivers.[10]

With the naming of each river, I see more and more
the limitations of my own historical consciousness,
the narrowness of my own interpretation of the
Enlightenment and the history of imagination since
that time. I think of Emille, the little girl sacrificed to
produce the bell that would guarantee the peace of
the ancient regime. The sounds of the bell and the
rivers "ancient as the world and older than the flow
of human blood in human veins" blend into one
mighty stream. Its current sweeps the depths of my
heart and lifts words from the favorite hymn of the
church in which I grew up:

When I tread the verge of Jordan,
Bid my anxious fears subside;
Death of death and hell's destruction,
Land me safe on Canaan's side.

But now these words are far more than a prayer for
my personal assurance in the face of death. The river
in my study is transforming the individualistic
meaning of my childhood song. The verge of Jordan
is the approach to the new world that is envisioned
by the oppressed. The anxious fears are my worries
about losing my faith under the influence of
postmodern theology, when in fact all I am losing is
an overly constricted imagination. The death of

death and hell's destruction is the death of all that
contorts the just purposes of God. And Canaan's side
is the new creation where no young girls are tossed
into the molten metal to make a bell for peace, and
where no angels need be sent to warn sleepy parents
to flee with their children the genocidal commands of
tyrants. By the power of the visionary imagination, I
am beginning to glimpse in new ways what the
ancient prophet declared:

> the glory of the Lord shall be
> revealed
> and all flesh shall see it together.
> (Isa. 40:5)

Notes

1. George Lakoff and Mark Johnson, *Metaphors We Live By*
(Chicago: The University of Chicago Press, 1980), p. 3.

2. Harry Emerson Fosdick, *The Modern Use of the Bible* (New York:
Macmillan, 1924), pp. 34-35. Emphasis added.

3. Phyllis Trible, *Texts of Terror: Literary-Feminist Reading of Biblical
Narratives* (Philadelphia: Fortress Press, 1984), p. 2.

4. Fosdick, *The Modern Use of the Bible,* p. 43.

5. Northrup Frye, *The Great Code: the Bible and Literature* (New
York: Harcourt Brace Jovanovich, 1981), p. xvii.

6. Robert McAfee Brown, *Unexpected News: Reading the Bible with
Third World Eyes* (Philadelphia: The Westminster Press, 1984), p. 14.

7. Lee Oo Chung, "One Woman's Confession of Faith." *New
Eyes for Reading: Biblical and Theological Reflections by Women from the
Third World,* eds. John S. Pobee and Barbel von Wartenberg-Potter
(Geneva: World Council of Churches, 1986), pp. 19-20.

8. Rosemary Radford Ruether, *Sexism and God-Talk: Toward a
Feminist Theology* (Boston: Beacon Press, 1983), p. 33.

9. Ibid., pp. 31-32.

10. Helen Vendler, ed., *The Harvard Book of Contemporary American
Poetry* (Cambridge, Mass.: Harvard University Press, 1985), p. 41.

CHAPTER 8

*R*eturn to the Source

I am suffering a malady that is common to all preachers: overdosing on words. This illness is not commonly discussed in the city of homiletical wisdom, but it ought to be. The best cure is an activity that is nonverbal. So I have turned to my flute and after a few scales begin to practice the solo treble accompaniment of a Bach aria that I am going to perform in a worship service.

The principles of the homiletical imagination are like the warm-up exercises on my flute. Just as scales and arpeggios prepare the way for inspired playing, so also the practice of being attentive with eye, body, and ear helps to sustain our creative preaching. Nevertheless, homiletical principles are never ends in themselves, and their mere application does not guarantee inspired preaching.

I continue practicing my flute, but my mind is not fully on the music. I am reflecting on the difference between the sermon that is perfectly crafted, but dead, and the sermon that is alive. Is there a homiletical principle that moves us beyond technique to the vital nerve of preaching?

Beyond Technique to the Vital Nerve

I put down my flute to catch my breath and gaze up through the skylight. The crown of the great silver maple tree that stands in my backyard is wreathed in fog this morning. It appears as if the mist were coming down from heaven instead of rising from the earth. I cannot tell whether I am looking upward to a great height or downward to a great depth.

Suddenly I hear a voice: "You better keep practicing if you are going to perform my music next week."

I pick up my flute and start playing the obligato to Bach's aria. The notes spill into the air, and the mist of sound that rises from the silver pipe in my hands blends with the cloud that approached from heaven. For as long as I play, Bach and I talk with each other.

He announces to me: "I have the homiletical principle you are looking for, and as a member of the great cloud of witnesses that Hebrews describes, I am going to preach the final sermon to you and to all the preachers who are reading this book. You have been talking about 'overdosing on words' and the need for preachers to take a rest from speaking. I can tell you from all my years in the organ loft, preachers do have a tendency to go on."

"I know they do, Bach. But tell me: how are you going to deliver a sermon?"

"You will play the flute, and I will preach through my music."

I explain to Bach: "Guest preachers are always introduced. What should I say about you?—'We are honored today to have as our preacher Johann Sebastian Bach, choir director and organist of St. Thomas's Church, Leipzig, composer of The St. Matthew Passion, The Mass in B Minor, The Art of the Fugue, The Brandenburg Concerti. . . . "

"No, no, that will not do at all. Where I am now, no one impresses anyone with his or her credentials."

"Wait a minute, Johann. Did I hear you say 'his or her'? Are you using inclusive language?"

"Of course, I am. We would not use anything else in the cloud. Don't you read your Bible? 'There is neither Jew nor Greek, there is neither slave nor free, there is neither male nor female; for you are all one in Christ Jesus.' In the cloud we live these words completely. You can tell them that in introducing my sermon."

I promise Bach that I will and then ask him: "What else do you want me to tell them?"

"I want you to explain my sermon outline to them, how carefully the music follows the poetic text:

And though with muted, feeble voices
the glory of the Lord be praised,
If [the] Spirit send the word on high,
then does it seem the loudest cry
that yet to heaven has been raised.[1]

Bach continued: "The verse answers your question about the difference between dead and living sermons. Preaching depends on the Spirit, and I make that point clear in my sermon. I am telling people with my music what I learned from a lifetime of composition: You may have perfected every method and technique, but without the Spirit the music is dead. And that is true for preachers as well. Their outline, their biblical interpretation, their use of language, their mastery of every homiletical rule and norm may all be polished, but only 'If [the] Spirit send the word on high' will the sermon sing and soar. I say this to all preachers: Follow the pull of the

Spirit to return to the Source, to God who made you and Christ who redeemed you. Understand all of your imaginative work as an effort to return to the Source."

"With Sighs Too Deep for Words"

I ask Bach, "Where did you get this idea for your sermon?"

"From Paul the apostle, who wrote: 'We do not know how to pray as we ought, but the Spirit's own self intercedes for us with sighs too deep for words.' All of us are familiar with these sighs, but not all of us listen to them. Yet, it is those sighs too deep for words that have lifted up the greatest music from my soul."

But Paul's words do not only apply to composers! Whatever our talent, if we listen in faith and in prayer, we can hear the Spirit sounding in our lives.

When someone we love more than we love ourselves is
with us
    we can hear the sigh . . . oooooo . . .
When we listen to the Emille bell
    tolling out the cries of the oppressed women
        we can hear the sigh . . . oooooo . . .
When our souls grow deep like the rivers which are
    "older than the flow of human blood in human
veins"
            and we realize our racism,
                we can hear the sigh . . . oooooo . . .
When the sleepy couple in the stable
    moves us to act for the rights of others
        we can hear the sigh . . . oooooo . . .
When we cringe at the injustice of our government

and a holy anger possesses us
 we can hear the sigh . . . oooooo . . .
When we go to our study to prepare our sermons
 and the brutality of this world weighs our hearts
  we can hear the sigh . . . oooooo. . . .

"All of these are the sighs of the Spirit," Bach stated, "and if we listen to them, we will hear God calling us—calling us to love, calling us to compassion, calling us to justice. This is why it is foolish to contrast the life of action with the life of prayer, silence, imagination, art, and music. In listening to the sighs of the Spirit, we receive power to do what is good and just and right. And when preachers attend to the sighs of the Spirit, their words take on the quality of heaven's voice and their speaking awakens in the listeners an awareness of the Spirit sighing within them."

All the time that Bach has been speaking I have been playing my flute. I come to the end of the aria and put down my instrument. There is an empty quiet to the room. I look out to the city beyond my dormer, then to the city of homiletical wisdom, and finally up through my skylight. The clouds have lifted now, and everything I gaze at is bathed in a single stream of pure and primal light. For a brief moment, heaven and earth shine with splendor upon splendor, and from my heart there arises a great long deep sigh . . . oooooo. . . . In that sigh I hear a prayer, asking that all of us who preach may renew our imaginations by returning to the Source, that with heart and soul and mind and strength we may listen to the One who is praying for us in sighs too deep for words . . . oooooo. . . .

Note

1. "And Though with Muted, Feeble Voices" from Cantata 36, *Schwingt freudig euch empor (Soar Joyfully on High)*.